Democracy and Political Violence

John Schwarzmantel

EDINBURGH UNIVERSITY PRESS

Edinburgh University Press Ltd
22 George Square, Edinburgh
www.euppublishing.com

Typeset in 11/14 Sabon by
Servis Filmsetting Ltd, Stockport, Cheshire, and
printed and bound in Great Britain by
CPI Antony Rowe, Chippenham and Eastbourne

A CIP record for this book is available from the British Library

ISBN 978 0 7486 3795 9 (hardback)
ISBN 978 0 7486 3796 6 (paperback)

Democracy and Political Violence

Contents

Preface and Acknowledgements

This book attempts to analyse the relationship between democracy and violence, looking at the topic from a perspective of what can be called 'applied political theory'. The aim is to present the ideals of democratic theory and see in what ways they are challenged by the phenomenon of political violence in both theory and practice. The book also seeks to look at ways in which liberal-democratic societies have responded to this challenge, and the problems faced by democratising societies when confronted with movements using political violence to achieve their aims. While the issues are presented in general terms, I have tried to illustrate them with examples taken from current politics world-wide, using cases from established democracies as well as from societies where democracy is something yet to be firmly implanted. The book also discusses attempts to assist the spread of democracy world-wide and the problems involved in attempts to promote democracy through outside intervention. The concluding arguments seek to offer an idea of the creation of democratic community as the most hopeful pathway to achieve a reduction in the use of violence as a political weapon.

In more detail, the plan of the book is as follows. The first chapter develops the idea that the ideal of democracy is a society in which violence would have no appeal, since processes of debate and compromise involving all citizens would make violence unnecessary as a means of political action. While conflict and antagonism are inevitable features of political life, the democratic ideal seeks to deal with conflict by establishing a community in which all its members are recognised as equally entitled to have their voice heard and their identity respected. Political and social exclusion and lack of recognition are presented as central factors in stimulating the recourse to political violence. The second and third chapters deal with the implications of political violence for the role of the state in liberal-democracy, and seek to analyse aspects of state violence. It is argued that seeing the challenge of violence as primarily a security problem creates the danger of extending the scope of state action towards an 'exceptional state' in which the security agencies of the state could have disproportionate power. In this way foundational values of the liberal-democratic state are endangered. The response should rather be, it is argued here, one of developing a more inclusive society which would render violence unnecessary and unattractive to all but an insignificant minority of its citizens.

The subsequent chapters seek to look further at agents and practices of political violence in contemporary politics. Chapter 4 suggests that terrorism is best seen as a perverted appeal to democratic principles, seeking to influence public opinion (a democratic principle) through the use of fear and violence, thus using illegitimate and extreme means to draw attention to grievances and problems of exclusion and non-recognition. Chapter 5 looks at nationalism as one very important cause of political violence. Nationalist groups resort to violence when they perceive that the state of which they are part fails to afford recognition to their particular national group. Nationalism therefore exemplifies the more general situation of exclusion and lack of recognition which fuels political violence. Chapter 6 returns to the theme of state violence, with respect to attempts to install democracy through outside intervention, and analyses these attempts from the perspective of democratic theory. The concluding two chapters move from 'diagnosis' to 'cure', in the sense that they seek to develop a concept of democratic community as the most hopeful response to the phenomenon of political violence. This section of the book argues for policies of institutional reform and a new discourse of politics as offering ways in which violence could be contained and steered into channels of democratic dialogue and peaceful resolution of inevitable conflicts and differences.

While dealing with these issues at a high level of generality evidently means 'painting with a broad brush', it is hoped that the treatment of the problem of democracy and violence in these pages provides a fruitful framework for thinking about the ways in which liberal-democratic societies could respond to one of the chief problems of our time. It is also hoped that the broad framework of analysis offered in what follows might be relevant to what are here called 'democracies in the making', and to all those seeking to establish or develop democracy in difficult situations of conflict and violent antagonism. I have taught for many years at the University of Leeds an MA module on the theme of 'Democratic Theory and Political Transformation', and also directed an MA programme in Democratic Studies which attracted students from around the world. This has been of great benefit in giving me a sense both of the value of democracy and also of the difficulty of establishing democracy in societies divided by conflict and antagonism. I am grateful to those students from a wide variety of countries who shared with me and with their fellow-students their aspirations towards a more democratic society for their country and for the world in general. Whatever the undoubted defects of the treatment of democracy and political violence in this book, I certainly believe that these are really important issues that concern all those in both established democracies as well as in 'democracies in the making' who wish to develop democracy further in their own society.

The democratic protests and opposition in Egypt, currently mobilising thousands of citizens, show the importance of the arguments articulated in this book for the need for democratic community. The demands of the protestors are focused on the demand for respect and recognition as citizens, and on the need for a regime which includes them as participants in a genuine democratic dialogue, and not as subjects of a dictatorial system.

Finally I must express my deep thanks to a number of friends whose support has been essential during the writing of this book.

My greatest debt is to Janet Wolff, who has been encouraging and positive from the very beginning when she commented incisively on the book proposal. I am also extremely grateful to David Beetham and Clare Woodford who read several draft chapters and who made very helpful suggestions for improvement and development of the ideas. I wish to thank my colleague Gabrielle Lynch for directing me to some of the literature on the violence which erupted in Kenya after the Presidential elections of December 2007. I am also grateful to my friend Judith Pallot for some encouragement and last-minute chivvying, both of which were much appreciated. My thanks are also due to my colleague Hendrik Kraetzschmar with whom I organised a seminar series for the Leeds University Centre for Democratisation Studies in the academic year 2008–9 on the theme of 'Democracy and Violence', and also to those colleagues who gave papers to that seminar series which provided much food for thought on the issues of the present book. David Cesarani provided some robust criticism, despite which I persevered in revising my manuscript. I am also happy to acknowledge with much gratitude and appreciation the help of Nicola Ramsey and her colleagues at Edinburgh University Press. I also wish to express my appreciation of the careful copy-editing work of Tim Clark, whose attention to detail greatly improved the typescript; I am most grateful for his efforts. Naturally none of those mentioned are in any way responsible for any defects, errors or weaknesses in the pages that follow.

John Schwarzmantel
Leeds, February 2011

1 Conflict and Community

Why do democratic societies today face challenges from those who resort to violence, and in what ways should the citizens and governments of such societies respond to these challenges? Under what conditions, nationally and internationally, is the use of violence necessary and legitimate to defend and spread democracy as a form of rule and protect democratic rights when they have been infringed? These broad questions form the subject of this book. By way of introduction some further presentation is necessary, given the wide nature of the subject-matter, and the fact that because of its topical nature it has been tackled in all sorts of ways by experts in security studies, in terrorism, as well as by those focusing on particular countries and areas of the world. In what ways can the present study, defined as an exercise in applied political theory, claim to offer a distinctive perspective? The term 'applied political theory' is meant to indicate the general approach taken here, which is to use certain basic ideas of democratic theory, explaining the ideals of democracy, and then to discuss in what ways those who use violence as a political weapon challenge those ideas. This is not to deny that in some cases, both historically and in the contemporary world, violence has been used not to oppose democracy, but as a way of extending it and gaining membership in a political community for those who are denied a voice in that community. For example, without the use or threat of political violence, it may be doubted whether the black majority in South Africa would have gained the right to exercise democratic rights in a system which entrenched the power of the white minority.

The Nature of Political Violence

No one tackling this subject in the present age can escape images and memories of 9/11, 11 September 2001, when terrorists attacked targets in the USA, unleashing violence against civilians in the 'twin towers', as well as against the Pentagon in Washington DC. These events in turn unleashed the 'war against terror', first in Afghanistan, and then in the invasion of Iraq, where the world's most formidable military machine was used to overthrow Saddam Hussein, even though he had nothing to do with the attacks of 9/11. Violence is practised not only by states, whether or not they are based on the principles of liberal-democracy, but also by non-state terrorist groups like Al Qaeda which oppose democracy, liberal or otherwise, and see the secular nature of liberal-democracy as an impious attempt to impose human will on a sphere that should be religious. Such groups have attacked liberal-democracy in violent terrorist ways, and again the images and memories are clear: the Madrid attacks of 2004 and the bombings in London of July 2005 showed that violent attacks on citizens in a liberal-democracy are a feature of contemporary politics, that we are living in a situation of 'society under siege' (Bauman 2002). In such a society violence or the threat of violence is continually present, exercised not only by terrorist groups who oppose both the policies and the basic principles of liberal-democracy, but also by agencies of the state who are charged with fighting terrorism and defending the security of the citizens of liberal-democracies. Indeed it seems as though violence is inseparable from the very nature of politics, since political struggle is carried on by state actors and non-state actors who are willing to use violence as a way of securing their ends. If violence can be defined as the employment or threat of physical coercion to achieve political ends, then it seems as if the sphere of the political is inseparable from the use (actual or threatened) of violent means. States and their agents impose physical coercion on those who break the law; non-state groups resort to violence if there seems no way in which they can achieve their ends through peaceful means of debate and discussion. Can violence be separated from politics? Could we ever aspire to a situation in which physical violence or its threatened deployment would not be a factor in political life? It would seem that this aspiration is one of an extremely idealistic, even utopian, kind.

However, the stance taken here starts from different presuppositions, and seeks to explore the relationship between democratic politics and the politics of violence in more optimistic ways which themselves challenge this view of the inseparability of democracy, or indeed of politics in general, from violence. This introduction sets out the broad perspectives and issues to be explored in what follows, with a view to providing a framework for the ensuing analysis. Following the title of the book, 'democracy and political violence', the chapter seeks to explain three core ideas – *democracy*, *violence*, and the nature of the *problems or challenges* which violence sets for democracy, and how those problems could be faced. To discuss these problems at a high level of generality may strike some readers as overly theoretical, but given that this is an exercise in applied political theory, the approach taken here has to spell out exactly the nature of the problem being addressed, and the general perspective which is to be the basis of the material treated.

Democracy as an ideal is here conceptualised as a system in which all members of the political community in question have an equal chance to participate in making the laws under which they live, whether directly or through representatives elected by and responsible to the citizen body. In terms of the issues which concern us here, a democratic system aspires to be one in which the issues on which citizens are divided can be settled by deliberation, debate and compromise, in other words by means which exclude the use of physical force or violence (the terms 'physical force' and 'violence' will be treated as synonymous). This perspective is similar to that used by Hannah Arendt in her discussion of violence and the distinction she employs between *violence* and *power*. In a recent analysis of Arendt's essay *On Violence*, the political theorist Iris Marion Young summarises Arendt's view of government in the following terms: 'Government ought to be the exercise of power as the expression and result of people coming together, assessing their problems and collective goals, discussing together how to deal with them, and persuading one another to adopt rules and policies, then each self-consciously acting to effect them' (Young 2007: 88). This is what a democratic polity aims at, in the present analysis: it seeks to achieve the exclusion of violence, and the substitution of cooperative and associative ways of public action (what Arendt calls 'power') in place of violence and coercion. Following Arendt again, violence emerges when such democratic associative power breaks down: 'Violence appears when power is in jeopardy', as she puts it (Arendt 1973: 122). A situation of violence would be one where 'might is right', where there is no agreement on procedures to decide issues on which there is disagreement and conflict, and where no central power exists to control those whose strength or physical force decides the issue. This state of affairs clearly evokes the 'state of nature' theorised by classical social contract theorists such as Hobbes or Locke, in which there can be no security for individuals, each of which is at the mercy of other individuals or groups who can use violence (brute strength and physical coercion) to get their way.

However idealistic it might sound, democracy aims at the exclusion of violence, through the substitution of consent and deliberation for physical force. Violence rules when democratic politics breaks down. It also threatens to dominate in the absence of a centralised state which can enforce rules and decision-making procedures on members of the political community, and when there is no agreement on what the political community is and who its members are. This implies that there has to be agreement on the territory and membership of the political community for a democratic society to exist and to function. If there are competing groups that do not recognise each other as citizens, each of whom is entitled to participate in common deliberative procedures, then democracy cannot function. In such a situation, violence is highly probable, since there is no agreement on the political space and the shared institutions through which deliberation could be carried on and compromise reached on issues which divide members of the political association. Hence the importance of issues of nationalism and national community for democracy and violence: if competing groups claim a particular territory as the territory of 'their' nation, and deny civic rights to members of other ethnic and national groups, then it is hard to see how violence can be averted and how a politics of democratic citizenship could be established.

Violence is thus defined here in a straightforward way as the use or threat of physical force to achieve political ends. But why do people resort to violence, and why is the attempt to create a democratic society in which debate, discussion and compromise replace violence and coercion so often problematic and unsuccessful? Why does violence occur? The following typology can be offered, as guiding the fuller analysis which comes in subsequent chapters. Violence occurs for the following reasons:

Hostility to the idea of democracy: If there are groups that see democracy – with its attendant procedures and principles of toleration of opposing points of view and a certain scepticism concerning the possibility of final truths in politics – as fundamentally illegitimate, then they will not accept democratic institutions and will seek to overthrow them in the name of some higher ultimate truth, whether religious or of some other nature. This category would clearly include those Islamic fundamentalists for whom democracy is a blasphemous system because it sees legitimate political authority stemming from 'the people' and invoking ideas of popular sovereignty, when this is seen as intrusion on the sphere of God, whose will must be supreme. However, there are other examples of such root-and-branch refusal of democratic principles and institutions. These could take more secular forms, seeking revolution through violent means, whether stemming from extreme right-wing movements seeking to institute (as German Fascism did) a *Volksgemeinschaft* or racially pure political community ruled by an all-powerful *Führer*, or from quite opposed Communist movements that aimed at the achievement of a more perfect 'people's democracy' free from the corruptions of bourgeois politics and the power of capitalist interests. In all these cases it could be said that violence stems from the rejection of pluralism, and the wish to impose by violent means a different system of unified values which rejects the pluralism, diversity and deliberation of liberal-democracy.

Demands for inclusion: A second answer to the question 'why do individuals and groups resort to violence?' is that *violence occurs as a response to exclusion and lack of recognition*. In such cases violence is the response of those who are excluded from the political system, or if not formally excluded see no chance of their interests as they define them being satisfied through the processes of 'normal' politics. In this case violence is used as a strategy, or as a means of calling attention to grievances which have not been attended to, for various reasons, by the political system as it is presently structured. Such violence could take the form of spontaneous or loosely organised urban riots, arising as a response to police brutality or social neglect and marginalisation; examples would be the US urban riots in the 1960s or, more recently (2005), the revolt of the French *banlieues*, especially in the Parisian region. Such violence could also take a more organised or structured form, expressed by movements which use violence strategically and rationally because they argue that their demands will not be met by a system in which they are in a permanent minority and their rights as democratic citizens repeatedly denied. The resort to violence in these cases is to be understood as a demand for democratic inclusion and recognition where these are not granted by the normal processes of democratic politics, and where there seems no prospect of securing such inclusion by means of deliberation and mutual recognition, seen here as the hallmarks of the democratic process.

Protest against nationalist oppression: A third reason is that violence is in many cases a response to nationalist oppression or foreign rule, occurring as a protest against such oppression or domination. Where there is a 'misfit' between state and nation, violence is often the strategy followed by groups who feel it is the only way to secure a situation in which state power is held by those who share the nationality and, in a broad sense, the culture of those subject to that state power. If a national group forms part of a state which does not reflect the identity of that national group, then violence is a distinct possibility. This possibility is heightened in cases where the minority national group feels that their identity is repressed and threatened by the state of which they are part. Even a degree of autonomy or regional self-government may be felt insufficient to secure the identity of state and nation which the nationalist group demands, so that violence is seen as the only means to achieve a proper 'fit' between state and nation. Examples of such nationalist violence are evident in the cases of Basque nationalism, the Kurds, Corsica, and the conflict in Sri Lanka between the Tamil Tigers and the government of Sri Lanka. The problem with such cases is that a solution along classical nationalist lines may only perpetuate the problem rather than solve it, since a secessionist solution which gives the minority national group a state of its own raises a new problem for minorities in the newly seceded state. For example, the Baltic states of what used to be the Soviet Union achieved the goal, as in Lithuania, Latvia and Estonia, of creating a state for 'their' particular national group. This, however, created a new problem for the Russian-speaking minorities in those newly independent nations, who found themselves in some cases discriminated against by language laws which made citizenship dependent on speaking the language of the new dominant national group. Nationalism, or rather the failure to recognise distinct national cultures, is therefore a clear factor in political violence, as used by groups who claim to speak for 'their' nation and redress a situation in which state power is held by those who are from a different national group and whose concerns do not reflect the identity of national minorities.

The above three categories refer to movements using violence *against* the state. However, any discussion of political violence has to recognise the use of *violence on the part of states themselves*, including democratic states. So, in addition to the three reasons for violence given above, two further categories of political violence can be identified, both of which involve the use of state power:

Violence by democratic states in defence of democracy in their own political arena: This is to be understood as the use of violence by the holders of state power in defence of democratic institutions and procedures against those individuals, groups and movements which are seen as threatening them. By the same token, this applies to the use of state power in 'transitional' situations, where state power is deployed against groups and movements that refuse to accept democratic procedures or any progress towards democracy, understood in the terms defined above as the acceptance of dialogue, discussion and compromise rather than physical force and the violent exclusion of certain categories of individuals from the status of citizenship. The purpose of the state, according to liberal-democratic theory, is to secure the safety of its citizens, and to use force where no other means will be effective. The problem here, clearly, concerns who decides what counts as a challenge to democracy, and what means are appropriate to meet such a threat. Democratic states have a range of possible tactics to respond to movements using violence for the three reasons identified above (hostility to democracy; demand for inclusion; protest against nationalist oppression or non-recognition). The response of a democratic state to violence can be to change its policy to meet the grievances expressed through violent action. Such a change in policy can emerge from a process of dialogue and negotiation out of which arises a solution acceptable to all parties, who agree to abandon the use of violence since there are now other non-violent ways in which their aims, or at least some of them, can be met. This seems to have been the scenario of the Good Friday agreement in Northern Ireland, which (on the whole successfully) offered a way out of the violent 'troubles'. Other responses of the state are less likely to offer a way out of violence: these include recourse to 'securitisation', in which the state extends the capacities and surveillance activities of its personnel to avert any threats against it. The obvious danger here is that such an extended process of 'securitisation' makes it likely that such increased surveillance will undermine rights and liberties characteristic of and foundational for the liberal-democratic order. Such activities on the part of the state do not represent a way of breaking the circle of violence, which can be intensified by mutual suspicion between the state and its citizens.

Another response on the part of the state, whether in an established democracy or a democracy 'in the making', is to establish its power by the use of overwhelming force, in an attempt to 'cleanse' the polity of those who use violence in pursuit of their aims. This has been the response of the Russian state to secessionist and nationalist movements in Chechnya. It also is exemplified by the situation in Sri Lanka, where the government used violence against the Tamil Tigers, and eventually won a military victory against them, thus 'removing' their violent challenge and establishing through massive force the conditions for civil peace and democratic procedures. There is an evident danger here that such unrestrained use of force in the name of defending or establishing democracy will fail in its purpose, by provoking anger and counter-violence on the part of those against whom state violence has been used in such extreme and unlimited ways. Even if such state violence proves effective, at least in the short term, it may breed such resentment and hostility that this is likely to create the grounds of further violent action rather than the basis for a democratic order. The use of violence by democratic states (established or 'in the making') is thus highly problematic for the reasons just given, and the examples to be discussed later in this book highlight further the difficulties involved in using violence in defence of democratic procedures.

Violence used by democratic states internationally: The recent period has witnessed the use of violence by liberal-democratic states and by international agencies in new and distinct ways. Violence in the form of war has been employed not in direct defence of democratic societies against outside aggression but in 'pro-active' ways aiming at 'regime change', supposedly to bring democracy to non-democratic societies. Furthermore, violence has been used for purposes of 'humanitarian intervention' with the avowed aim of protecting human rights (civil rights, democratic rights and basic rights of the person) where these have been infringed by the governments of such non-democratic societies. The obvious examples here are those of Afghanistan and Iraq, but equally intervention in Kosovo was justified by a supposedly new doctrine of 'humanitarian intervention'. Such a doctrine holds that where a government cannot guarantee democratic rights and abide by democratic procedures, the international community has both a right and a duty to enforce such rights and procedures. Acceptance of such ideas inevitably involves the use of violence, since in such cases the state acting in violation of democratic rights will not peacefully accept interference with its power over its own territory. Humanitarian intervention is thus by definition violent intervention, involving the use of force to secure democratic rights and human rights against governments who violate those norms. The problems of this type of violence are equally evident: while carried out in the name of democracy, it involves agents other than those of the states and of citizens of the countries where such interventions take place. Democratic principles call for the self-rule of the citizens, who themselves should exercise and maintain the procedures which allow them to make the laws under which they live. In the cases envisaged here, however, the citizens of these societies are by definition unable to exercise such democratic rights, which thus have to be supported or implemented by an outside force, whether that of particular liberal-democratic states or international agencies in cooperation with such states.

The problem for democratic theory, and for the 'applied political theory' developed here, is that on the one hand the principles of democracy seem to argue against any intervention by forces outside the community in question. This is because the assertion of democratic rights should, at least in the first instance, be the responsibility and task of those claiming them for themselves. Moreover, the danger of outside intervention is that it brings with it the risk of a form of paternalism. Outside forces claim to know what is in the true interests of those they are liberating. Beyond that, such outside forces (the agents of humanitarian intervention) are not 'innocent' or free from their own partial interests, both economic and political. This is especially true if those agents are particular states, since they have their own agendas and concerns, not just for their security (seen as threatened by the non-democratic regimes) but for economic interests (command over oil resources, for example). Such violence supposedly conducted in the name of democratic principles thus contradicts some of the bases of those democratic principles invoked in support of humanitarian intervention.

On the other hand, defenders of such intervention could point to stronger principles of democracy, which would entail adopting a cosmopolitan perspective: democracy and human rights are not restricted to particular territories of sovereign nation-states, but are universal rights for which the world community (however that is defined) is responsible. Democracy in established democracies is threatened if certain areas of the world are left excluded from the benefits of democratic politics, since such areas can be used as safe havens for movements targeting established democracies. This is the justification currently offered for Western involvement in Afghanistan. If citizens (or would-be citizens) are denied their democratic rights through violent repression on the part of their own government, then democratic principles, seen in a cosmopolitan perspective and invoking ideas of a 'global community of citizens' (Archibugi 2008), impose on all those capable of pursuing it a right of assistance to secure a democratic polity. Hence violent intervention is legitimised in the name of establishing a democratic polity and securing democratic rights.

Democracy and Violence

If what has been said so far outlines a typology of forms of violence, the next task must be to explain further the nature of the challenge which violence, as defined above, presents to the ideals and realities of democratic politics in the context of contemporary liberal-democratic societies, as well as in societies where democratic institutions and forms of life have not been established. These problems relate to the role that violence plays as a threat to the working of democratic institutions, and as a tool employed by democratic governments to defend themselves against that threat.

This book deals with three fundamental questions, which can be set out as follows. The first is to identify the nature of the problem which violence poses for democratic politics today. In what ways are liberal-democratic societies threatened by those who do not accept democratic procedures and institutions, and is there anything novel about such a threat? Does violence represent a new attack on democracy, and in what ways is violence incompatible with democratic ideals?

The second question, equally ambitious, concerns the causes of political violence: is it possible to arrive at any generalisations which might explain why certain individuals and groups resort to violence and reject the politics of discussion and compromise, mediated through appropriate institutions? Such processes of rational dialogue are fundamental to the nature of the liberal-democratic order. As we have touched upon already, one crucial idea here is that of exclusion. Violence in many cases arises when a minority is excluded from some of the institutions of liberal-democracy and denied the mutual respect between citizens that should characterise a democratic society – though this does not exhaust the causes which lead people to use violence for political ends.

This then leads on to the third question, which focuses on ways in which violence as a factor in political life might be tamed, contained, or even excluded as a significant element in the political life of democratic societies. If we can understand the nature of political violence and in broad terms the factors that stimulate or underlie it, then this clearly has implications for policies designed to steer violence into the channels of peaceful discussion and rational debate. It is no doubt highly idealistic to think that violence could ever be totally eradicated from political life. However, if the threat that violence poses to the security of citizens can be reduced, then the gap between the ideal of a democratic society and the reality of contemporary politics could be diminished, so that on a national as well as a global level the prospects of a healthy and flourishing democracy could be encouraged. The approach employed here uses the tools of social science to illuminate these problems, by combining political theory and more empirical political science, in the belief that the task of social science is to contribute to the discussion and possible resolution of urgent practical political and social problems. In order to achieve this ambitious goal, it is clearly necessary to specify more explicitly what the problem of democracy and violence is in contemporary times, and to suggest a theoretical framework which could offer a rewarding way of approaching the problem.

What exactly is meant by violence and in what ways is the problem of its relationship to democracy a new one? Violence has always been present in political life. Politics by definition is an attempt to contain and manage violence, which could never be totally eradicated from human affairs. Violence can be defined simply as the use of physical force to achieve one's ends. In that sense violent action abandons any attempt to convince others through the force of the better argument, or through appeals to authority. Instead it operates through fear – fear of physical harm being inflicted on those who do not comply with the demands of those using violent means. In the vivid words of Judith Butler: 'To the extent that we commit violence, we are acting on another, putting the other at risk, causing the other damage, threatening to expunge the other' (Butler 2004: 29). She describes violence as 'surely a touch of the worst order, a way a primary human vulnerability to other humans is exposed in its most terrifying way' (Butler 2004: 28). Violence occurs in all dimensions of life, both public and private. *Domestic* violence is commonly used within the family to maintain male or patriarchal power over women and children. *Criminal* violence is used to achieve personal gain through robbery or physical intimidation, or through the infliction of bodily harm on those opposing the will of the criminal. The focus of the present discussion is on *political* violence, defined in quite straightforward terms as the infliction of physical harm on individuals, or the threat to do this, in the pursuit of some political goal. A political goal can be distinguished from a private one in that the aim to be pursued through the use of violence is some change in the overall nature and structure of society, whether that involves a change in position of some group within it, or the nature of the laws, values and norms which govern that society. An act of violence directed towards individual gain is not an act of political violence. By contrast an act by a group or individual which calls on the society to change its structure, its laws or its way of life falls within the definition of the term 'political violence', since it employs the threat or the commission of acts of physical coercion and intimidation as a means to achieve those ends.

The perspective on violence offered here is thus one which focuses on violence as practised by identifiable agents, rather than a more nebulous concept of 'systemic' violence. These agents may be agents of the state, or private actors. The aim of the state (in theoretical terms) is to preserve a monopoly of violence in order to assure the safety and security of its citizens. In a democratic state, the use of violence is meant to be controlled and limited, so as to ensure that the exercise of physical coercion is legitimate, used only as a necessary weapon to defend the democratic order against those who would challenge it, themselves using violent means. But how can democratic societies properly police and control the means of violence in order to keep it within those legitimate limits? And who decides when violence is necessary and justified? Rejecting a vague concept of systemic violence may make it easier to resolve these questions, since the focus here is on acts of physical coercion (or the threat to use coercion) carried out by identifiable agents or persons, whether operating on behalf of or against the state. The definition of violence employed here, focusing on political as opposed to domestic or criminal violence, is thus one which confines the phenomenon to acts of physical coercion, consciously carried out by particular persons with an aim that can be articulated. That purpose might be to secure the democratic system against destabilising attacks, or it might be to transform or overthrow the democratic system and install a new way of life, as seems to be the goal of so-called Islamic fundamentalists who aim at eradicating secularism and imposing one particular version of Islam. Other acts of violence aim to secure recognition and respect for those who are excluded from full membership of democratic society.

Violence as a political weapon has been used in the past as well as in contemporary conditions to secure membership of the democratic political community for those denied a place within it. Debates in the Chartist movement between adherents of 'physical force' and 'moral force' illustrate historically that these are not exactly new issues (Chase 2007). They provide an example of the use of violence in order to attain democratic rights, when channels of peaceful action are closed off by the holders of political power. Thus political violence in the perspective taken here involves acts of physical coercion in pursuit of some political goal, which can be expressed in a public way. Violence also arises on the part of groups or individuals who are formally and legally members of the political community, but who are not afforded the recognition and the full social benefits which membership of the political community is intended to provide. In this sense the recourse to violence is a demand for recognition and respect, an appeal for rights to be respected in reality rather than merely in a formal sense. In conditions of economic crisis and of severe inequality, such violent protests against the existing state of things can be expected to increase, if the formal channels of political power do not afford recognition of these inequalities and offer some means of redress.

This approach to the question does not make any distinction between the terms 'force', 'violence' or 'coercion', which are seen as synonymous. Violence can be used in defence of the existing order, as well as being a means of opposing it. As the title of one recent study makes clear, *When States Kill* (Menjivar and Rodríguez 2005), violence is certainly not the exclusive preserve of movements acting against the state. The state itself is a violent actor, both directly and when it 'out-sources' or encourages the use of violence by favoured non-state actors, as indicated by the term of 'state-sponsored terror'. The use of state violence in a democracy requires checks and controls, to avoid the danger of undermining those rights and values which are fundamental to the democratic order. The use of violent means by those opposing the state involves questions of inclusion and exclusion, and requires careful distinctions: are those employing violence doing so as an appeal to be included as full members of a democratic society? Or, if such inclusion has already been formally achieved, are they demanding that it comes along with proper respect, recognition and participation in the goods and benefits of citizenship on equal terms with other citizens? In such cases, violence is exercised by those who feel that it is the only means of drawing attention to their grievances, when all other channels are closed down. This needs to be distinguished from the violence employed by groups who do not adhere to the values and institutions of democratic society, but who engage in violence either for its own sake, or as a means to annihilate or overthrow democratic structures and values. Analysing the nature of violence in democratic societies thus involves distinguishing between the different justifications offered in its defence, as well as differentiating state and state-sponsored violence on the one hand from violence used by those opposing the state, and the diverse forms of the latter. There can be violence *for* as well as *against* democracy. Part of the problem for social science, and for those dealing with this question as practitioners of politics, is that a blanket definition and a sweeping approach to the problem are not helpful ways of tackling the question. The agents of violence differ, as do the justifications offered in defence of such political violence.

Violence is incompatible with democracy in the sense that the use of physical coercion cannot be reconciled with the values of rational discourse among equal citizens which are basic to the democratic way of life. Yet democracy can itself produce violence, especially when understood in simplistic 'majoritarian' terms, as 'the rule of the majority'. This is of course an impoverished and inadequate view, since democracy involves more than the rule of the largest sector of society. If the body of democratic citizens is divided by ethnic or cultural markers, and one cultural or ethnic group is in a permanent minority, then democracy understood (however inadequately) as majority rule can foster the violent persecution of the minority by the majority. This is what Michael Mann correctly identifies as 'the dark side of democracy', when '*ethnos*' becomes '*demos*', in other words when the majority define themselves as a closed ethnic group denying civic rights to those of a different ethnic identity (Mann 2005). This is one way in which the question of democracy and violence has become more salient in contemporary times, linked with the problems of multiculturalism and identity politics. Some of the classic formulations of democratic political theory were devised for a 'simpler' time (Bobbio 1987: 37), when democratic politics was envisaged as being carried on by citizens not divided by cultural or ethnic markers. In contemporary conditions this is less likely to be the case. The divisions that emerge in a democratic society, arising inevitably out of political differences which surface in any complex society, often take on an ethnic or a cultural form, leading to violence rather than the peaceful reconciliation of conflict which is the ideal of a democratic community of citizens. Democracy in practice, far from being at the opposite pole from violence, may in some of its forms stimulate and provoke violence, and thus in addition to state, state-sponsored, and anti-state forms of violence, we have to consider 'democratic violence', or violence provoked by the very mechanisms of democracy itself, when majority rule is exercised in conditions of fear and insecurity experienced by a minority group.

Violence and the State

In what ways is this question of violence 'new'? Does it have features in contemporary society which make it different from those which it had in the past? The problem of political violence is the oldest one of political life: the activity of that central political institution, the state, is a constant attempt to contain, restrict or exclude violence from pervading everyday life. It was Hobbes who gave classical expression to this perspective, when he contrasted the 'state of nature' with the situation where the 'Leviathan' of the state could provide security for its members. In the state of nature, people live in a constant state of fear, subject to physical force or the threat of violence which is impossible to avoid (Hobbes 1968). Only through handing over their natural rights to the state can security and freedom from violence be achieved. Thus in this perspective the state uses its power to restrict and contain violence. This end is to be achieved by concentrating the legitimate use of violence in the hands of the state, whose agents are empowered to employ it against private persons who themselves act or seek to act in coercive ways.

If the state aims at the control of violence in order to ensure the security of its citizens and its exclusive hold on the means of coercion, why is violence a particular problem in contemporary politics? One answer to this question focuses on the diminishing power of the liberal-democratic nation-state, faced with movements and identities which on a global level escape the control of state power. In our time the situation seems highly paradoxical: in liberal-democratic societies, the state and its surveillance capacities seem an omnipresent reality, not just through closed-circuit cameras which track every move people make, but through the accumulation of data in the hands of the state. Surveillance is a key term in the vocabulary of contemporary politics, giving agents of the state greater opportunities for regulating the behaviour of its citizens. Yet the organising or regulatory powers of the nation-state have weakened, so that its hold over the violent tendencies of some of its citizens seems increasingly tenuous. If the state's monopoly of power is less complete, then violence will be more prominent as a feature of contemporary politics, precisely because the state is weaker in its control over those who wish to challenge it, for whatever reason. Zygmunt Bauman talks of 'the emaciated sovereignty and waning powers of the state' (Bauman 2002: 11) and points to 'the ever more evident, and perhaps irretrievable, loss of the privileged (and *unassailably* superior) position enjoyed or claimed by the nation-state' (Bauman 2002: 8).

If this perspective is correct, then it seems to establish the paradox that in an age of greater surveillance and the pervasiveness of state power, the state becomes weaker, despite the growing sophistication of the tools at its disposal. There has been a privatisation of violence, comparable to the way in which many of the economic and social functions previously exercised by the state have also been abandoned, intentionally or otherwise, and ceded to actors uncontrolled by structures of democratic politics. This might apply particularly to weak or failing states, like contemporary Pakistan (Rashid 2008) where the central government is unable to control violent groups who use part of the territory of the state to carry out acts of violence directed against other states, in the name of religious fundamentalism. But it could also apply to more established nation-states where violent groups are able to act as economic entrepreneurs and impose their own rules of conduct and their own violent norms, as vividly described in a recent study of the Camorra in and around Naples (Saviano 2008).

These seem extreme examples, but the problem of political violence and its relationship to democracy is more extensive. Democracy in the fullest sense should exclude violence and render it unnecessary, since the ideal of democracy aims at the reconciliation of conflicting interests and values through debate, discussion, compromise and, where possible, consensus. This ideal rejects a Hobbesian Leviathan state accepting the surrender of citizens' rights in order to create security for its citizens and take whatever measures are necessary to maintain that security. A democratic society should achieve a degree of community and solidarity through the genuine involvement of all its members in making the laws under which they live. Democracy further involves an acceptance of citizens' diverse and distinct identities, that is, an idea of mutual respect and recognition among citizens, where each is equally entitled to the benefits of living in a political community.

As we have seen, where that acceptance is lacking, those who are not afforded full recognition as citizens may have recourse to violence as a weapon. This invites consideration of how democratic societies, world-wide, can extend social and political inclusion so as to render such recourse to violence unnecessary, giving priority to the use of 'ballots' rather than 'bullets.'

The problem of political violence is thus not a new one: politics has been concerned in all societies with the Hobbesian question, identified as such by the sociologist Talcott Parsons, of 'how is social order possible?' (Parsons 1968: 89). Citizens of established liberal-democratic societies today have a greater chance of escaping violence than in the past, when even normal journeys across their territory were perilous enterprises. Yet how does this account for the perception that we live in more insecure times, and that violence is now more of a problem than in the past? Different protagonists or agents of violence have emerged, using distinct forms of politics appropriate to a global age and to the emergence of a different form of state. This seems to be the key idea of Philip Bobbitt's recent analysis in *Terror and Consent*, in which he suggests that the emergence of what he calls 'the market state' has created more opportunities for terrorism, defined by him as 'the use of violence to advance a political agenda by preventing persons from doing what they would otherwise lawfully do' (Bobbitt 2008: 530). Bobbitt argues that contemporary politics is marked by the transition from the nation-state to the 'market state'. While the nation-state based its legitimacy on improving the material life-conditions of its citizens, the so-called market state seeks to maximise individual opportunity. It outsources many functions, and relies more on ideas of choice. The result is that 'the threatening nature of the transition from the nation state to the market state invites violence' (Bobbitt 2008: 92), and makes it easier for terrorist groups to acquire weapons of mass destruction.

This line of analysis suggests that terrorist networks, using violence as a political weapon, imitate the market state which in a way gives such networks greater opportunities. Weapons, including weapons of mass destruction, become commodities like everything else, to be bought and sold on the world market. A new type of state, and indeed a different form of society, create new opportunities for their citizens while extending such opportunities to those who would oppose the state by exploiting its more open and fluid nature. As the state changes its nature and relinquishes its hold over citizens by opening up new areas for individual choice, leaving a large sphere of decision-making to the sphere of the market, this also opens up new opportunities for terrorists and practitioners of violence. The collective infrastructure is more vulnerable. In Bobbitt's words, 'the dramatic growth in wealth and productivity that is harnessed by the market state has as its concomitant a parallel growth in vulnerability' (Bobbitt 2008: 97).

This suggests that the emergence of a new form of state has the result that the perennial problem of political violence is itself transformed. If the state withdraws from or privatises aspects of life, or leaves them to the forces of the market in ways which were unthinkable for the traditional nation-state, then this creates the possibility that these market forces can be bought (in a literal sense) by groups intent on using violence for their own political ends, whether they be Bin Laden's Al Qaeda or the Neapolitan Camorra. In a similar way Bauman talks about a 'planetary frontier-land' exemplifying a new situation of global disorder: 'the perpetuation of global disorder suits the purposes of the terrorists as well as it serves the world domination of those who wage war against them' (Bauman 2002: 93). If the domination of 'traditional' nation-states is no longer so secure, then this opens the field for practitioners of violent politics who flourish in a new 'global space' un-policed by any agency able to impose order on this frontier-land. The problem of political violence and of the challenges it presents to democracy has taken on new forms, which are both global and networked in character. Any attempt to offer answers to the question of how violence might be 'steered' into the channels of peaceful discussion and compromise has to respond in terms which are not limited to the nation-state, and which take account of these new networked and more 'liquid' types of political violence.

Community and Conflict

In what ways are contemporary democratic societies challenged by violent politics, and what is meant by the key terms in this antithetical relationship, 'democracy' and 'violence'? It is regrettably easy to answer the first part of this question. There is plenty of evidence that violence is an ever-present problem for democracies, in both established democracies and in societies in the process of transition towards democracy. The obvious examples which overshadow contemporary politics are those of 11 September 2001, and the bombings in Madrid and London of 2004 and 2005 respectively. But there are other conflicts in Western liberal-democracies which have expressed themselves in violence: for example, the nationalist conflicts in Northern Ireland and in the Basque country. While recent political science literature has cast some doubt on the applicability of the concept of 'transition', especially if it denotes an irreversible teleological progression from authoritarian rule to a fully fledged democracy (Carothers 2002), violence has also erupted in societies which have sought to move towards democracy, for example in the violence which accompanied the break-up of Yugoslavia, giving birth to the concept of 'ethnic cleansing'. Rwanda, Sudan, and religious and ethnic conflicts in Lebanon all provide further relevant examples. However, the emphasis in what follows is on what can be called established liberal-democracies, and the ways in which they seek to contain violence. The discussion also seeks to deal with the ways in which contemporary liberal-democracies, particularly the United States, have sought to implant democracy and create it 'from outside' in the notable examples of Iraq and Afghanistan. In the contemporary world, democratic societies are involved with the politics of violence in two ways: as *objects* of attack from those who use the politics of violence, and as *subjects* employing violence themselves to defend the democratic order, and also in many cases to spread liberal-democracy in areas of the world inhospitable to democratic ideals.

The general theoretical framework which might illuminate such problems rests on two broad themes: *community* and *conflict*. Both are necessary for a democratic society to flourish, yet each can give rise to violence which undermines its working. A democratic society needs a sense of solidarity between and among its members, who should see themselves as sharing membership of a community of citizens, bound together by a sense of mutual obligation, with common rights of citizenship. The problem for contemporary democratic societies is how to achieve democratic community under conditions of 'deep diversity', where the bonds between citizens are weaker than they once were. Democracy thus requires community, and agreement on the question of who its members are. Yet community can erupt into violence if its citizens seek to heighten their sense of solidarity and identity at the expense of some outsider group or section of society held to be not truly part of the community. On the part of the minority 'outsider' group, violence can develop if such a group is unable to gain access to the centres of decision-making, or if the institutions of the 'mainstream' society do not afford such minority groups sufficient respect or recognition.

The problem of violence in contemporary liberal-democratic societies is thus intrinsic to the very nature of democracy as such. A democratic society can only function if there is agreement on the boundaries of citizenship, on the question of who forms the citizen body. Yet there are different ways of forming the criteria for such democratic community: if the concept is one of ethnic community as the basis for democracy, then this is often purchased at the expense of some out-group, whose identity is seen as a challenge to the identity of the majority group. This is the problem with making a concept of national solidarity the basis of a community of citizens, since such solidarity is often expressed in opposition to the non-nationals, seen as potentially undermining the unity of the nation.

The requirements for democratic community in the contemporary world are thus at one and the same time more difficult to fulfil, and more necessary than ever. They are more problematic because of the increased salience of difference, and the fact that any degree of cultural homogeneity has diminished within the framework of particular nation-states. What is required as a prerequisite for the healthy functioning of democratic society can slide all too easily into a phenomenon which undermines democracy itself. The satisfaction of the need for democratic community leads to violence if such an association is seen as a group defined by certain 'markers' which have to be affirmed through the victimisation of some group lacking those defining characteristics which form the criteria of citizenship. Such criteria are often those of culture and sometimes too of ethnicity, usually linked to a shared national history. This makes the assertion or affirmation of a 'pre-political' community a firm basis for democratic community. This has led Ghia Nodia, for example, to affirm that the concept of the nation is but another name for 'We the People', and Margaret Canovan to argue, convincingly, that some idea of the nation is like the 'battery' which powers a democracy, even though that battery may be ignored by many democratic theorists (Nodia 1994; Canovan 1998). Such arguments maintain that the idea of a community of citizens, to use Dominique Schnapper's phrase, is best expressed by a concept of the civic nation, through which citizens are linked to each other not by ethnicity but by the shared possession of common political rights (Schnapper 1994).

The problem, however, is that such a political concept of the nation rests – in ways that are often hidden and implicit rather than explicit – on a non-civic or more emotional bond of a shared history and culture, from which it is difficult to divorce the more abstract and perhaps 'soul-less' concept of what Habermas calls 'constitutional patriotism' (Habermas 1996: 500). Such a civic identity is linked to the state rather than the nation. National community, on the other hand, often rests on more emotional and ethnic roots, which raises the danger of a slippage into hostility and even violence against those who are seen not to share the same cultural and historical identities. Democracy thus turns into its opposite, and the fostering of a 'community of citizens' leads to violent actions directed against those seen as outside the community, even though they may be living on the same territory as those who assert their own identity and seek to affirm it in reaction against those who are not 'one of us'.

Conflict and Anger

While democracy is a political system which in its ideal form excludes violence and renders it unnecessary as a political tool, in reality this ideal is far from realisation. The contemporary German philosopher Peter Sloterdijk has drawn our attention to the significance of 'anger' as a factor in politics in his book *Zorn und Zeit* (Anger and Time) (Sloterdijk 2006). According to his analysis, in the pre-modern age anger was seen as something almost holy, something bound up with heroic action, through which the gods of the ancient world interfered in the workings of human society. His analysis seeks to show how in the modern era a range of political movements has drawn on what he calls the 'anger bank' – the deposits of anger inevitably stored up in any society – exploiting it for particular political purposes. However, while Sloterdijk's arguments are helpful in identifying anger as a motivating force for political action, it seems doubtful that there is a fixed quantum or deposit of anger in all societies. The task of social science is rather to investigate what social and political factors contribute to this anger, and to debate the conditions under which anger and its ensuing violence could be reduced and steered into the channels and institutions of democratic debate and compromise.

The second requirement of democracy, *conflict*, seems to contradict that of community. In any complex society, conflict is both an inescapable feature and at least to some degree a desirable one. In any society other than the most basic and simple there will be different views on how political life should be organised, on what policies should be adopted and on the nature of the desirable society. Debate and discussion through peaceful means is an integral part of a democratic society and in part defines what democracy is. Uniformity and total agreement on all aspects of social life would lead to the dull conformity which liberal theorists like John Stuart Mill rightly saw as the death of progress and intellectual stimulation. Politics is about conflict, and the political process arises from the inevitable nature of conflict and difference. In the words of Ralph Miliband, 'all concepts of politics, of whatever kind, are about conflict – how to contain it, or abolish it. What is specific about Marxist politics is what it declares the nature of the conflict to be; and what it proclaims to be its necessary outcome' (Miliband 1977: 17). Yet, as this quotation suggests, views of politics other than Marxism are equally in agreement that politics in a general sense arises out of the necessary conditions of discord and division or of factions. In *The Federalist Papers*, to take one famous example, Madison put it as follows: 'The latent causes of faction are thus sown in the nature of man, and we see them everywhere brought into different degrees of activity, according to the different circumstances of civil society' (Madison, Hamilton and Jay 1987 [1788]: 124).

If conflict cannot be eradicated as part of the condition of humans living in society, the distinctiveness of the democratic method is to seek to resolve those differences by peaceful, i.e. non-violent processes, in which violence becomes unnecessary or even unthinkable, because it is rejected by all members of society as a legitimate means of pursuing their interests. The ideals of democracy thus have built into them a view of human beings as capable of being moved by rational argument rather than brute force. Violence is condemned because it treats human beings as physical objects: it devalues reason because those who engage in violent action get their way through exploiting fear of injury or death, not through a process in which individuals or groups recognise each other as rational interlocutors in a dialogue. Thus the aim of democratic politics is to exclude the recourse to violence because of its dehumanising effects. The idea of democracy is based on an idea of mutual respect and recognition of others as equal rational beings, rather than as enemies with whom there can be no dialogue, only fighting. On this view, then, democracy and violence are mutually exclusive terms: where there is a fully inclusive democracy there should be no violence, since democracy means exactly the renunciation of violence in favour of those processes of dialogue and discussion which lead to reconciliation of difference through compromise. If individuals or groups are certain that their voice will be heard so that their interests will be taken into account and to some extent acted on, then there is no reason for them to have recourse to violence, the outcomes of which are so unpredictable and hazardous, even for the physically stronger person. As Hobbes classically pointed out in Chapter XIII of *Leviathan*: 'For as to the strength of body, the weakest has strength enough to kill the strongest, either by secret machination, or by confederacy with others, that are in the same danger with himselfe' (Hobbes 1968 [1651]: 183). The democratic method is thus based on two kinds of consideration, ethical and practical. Democratic citizens renounce violence because it devalues human beings by overriding their capacity and will for rational argument. Violence can never produce any security since it entails a colossal expenditure of energy and effort for no certain return.

Clearly this democratic exclusion of violence is an ideal, not a reality. It rests on various presuppositions that are unlikely to be fulfilled in the real world. First, it relies on the assumption that all interests and perspectives are in fact taken into account in the political system in question, and that therefore no one person or group will feel the need to have recourse to violence outside established constitutional channels in order to make their voice heard. Second, the implication is that all political actors accept the premise that violence degrades the status of the human actor, or that it is possible and desirable to resolve conflict through democracy, and that this is ethically superior to means of violent conflict. If someone believes that there is something inherently ennobling about violence, or that their own goal is an 'all or nothing' one on which there can be no compromise, or that the possible interlocutors in the democratic dialogue are not worthy of respect or of being listened to, then such considerations will make the democratic aspiration to exclude violence impossible to realise in practice.

However, even apart from such considerations, the total exclusion of violence through democratic procedures is impossible to realise in practice and does not work in the pure sense described above. Democratic politics does not exclude violence, but seeks rather to control it and use it for its own purposes. Max Weber's famous definition of the state is relevant here: 'a state is a human community that (successfully) claims the monopoly of the legitimate use of physical force within a given territory . . . The state is considered the sole source of the "right" to use violence' (Weber 1970 [1919]: 78). Weber was here analysing the state in general, but evidently his remarks include the democratic state: like any other state, the democratic state exercises violence and claims the right to do so. It has to use violence (or at least the threat of violence) to maintain itself as a state. One can suggest two ways in which the justified use of violence is specific to the democratic state. First, in the establishment of democracy, the state has to repress those who are not willing to 'lay down their arms' and accept democratic procedures. If it does not do this, then democracy can never be established, and the politics of permanent violence or of undemocratic rule will continue. One example of this was the establishment of democracy in post-apartheid South Africa: in reaction to sections of the white minority who refused to abide by the result of majority rule, or who threatened to take violent action to impede a democratic election, the democratic state or the agents of democratic transition were justified in using coercion against them in order to prevent their disruption of democratic procedures. In this case there were sufficient elements of a democratic state present, with adequate control over the means of coercion, to deploy this threat of violence against those who intended to prevent the installation of the democratic order. The threat of violence was here necessary to achieve the establishment of a democratic regime.

The second case in which the exclusion of violence from democracy breaks down is the use of violence to defend democracy against its enemies, as in the case of an established liberal-democratic society threatened by a group which does not accept the democratic 'rules of the game'. This differs from the first case only in that what is involved is a democratic system which is 'up and running', as opposed to one in the process of being established. However, the use of violence to defend democracy may itself undermine democracy since the means used may themselves violate democratic norms. This may result from empirical rather than philosophical considerations, especially if it is the security services themselves who are entrusted with taking the decisions in this area. Even assuming that they are committed to maintaining and not eroding democratic processes, such branches of the state may well have a professional or bureaucratic interest in exaggerating the scope of the threat, if only to demand greater resources for their activities. If they do so and thus cast their net more widely, this infringes upon the democratic nature of the state they are supposed to be preserving and defending. The struggle to defend democracy thus risks leading to the erosion of democracy.

It is thus clear that democratic states employ violence both to establish themselves and also to guarantee their continued stability. The dilemma is that in so doing they may undermine or erode their own ethos and singular way of life. The state becomes suspicious of its citizens who themselves come under greater surveillance, with the whole process justified in the name of preserving democracy from threat. The themes raised here are those of what one writer calls 'militant democracy', which 'shrinks the scope of political rights by refusing to extend them to those who seek to use democratic means toward non-democratic ends' (Rosenfeld 2006: 44). Such 'militancy' with regard to the perceived enemies of democracy entails a willingness to override the rights of those who appear to ignore or oppose democratic 'reasonableness'. Damian Chalmers writes of the danger of a 'new form of political reason' emerging, in which the existing order is defended just as it is: a form of market society in which those who are seen as not fitting in are treated differently from those who are full citizens. The fight against terrorism is used as the excuse or pretext for this discriminatory treatment. In Chalmers' words: 'If one looks at the central actions taken in the war on terror, they have been to protect the European Union market society' (Chalmers 2006: 71). If violence is necessary for the establishment or preservation of democracy, what are the permissible limits of the exercise of that violence, and the processes by which they to be scrutinised and secured? One example can be taken from Spanish politics in the 1990s, when the then Spanish Prime Minister, Felipe González, was accused of authorising terrorist action on the part of state agencies against GAL, itself a violent organisation threatening the state (Woodworth 2002). If democratic politics extends the scope of violent action (or its threat), what then happens to the aspiration towards the exclusion of violence from the terrain of democratic politics? Furthermore, what are the criteria according to which certain groups (or individuals) are to be seen as 'enemies of democracy', against whom the threat of violence can be justifiably employed? Here again there is a danger of slippage, through the extension of the category of suspects to ever larger sections of the population.

Inclusion and Exclusion

The exclusion of violence from democratic politics rests on the assumption that all groups have equal access to those channels of democratic politics which make violence unnecessary. This assumes that the kind of conflict inevitable in a pluralistic society can be handled by compromise and discussion through which, to some degree, all parties find satisfaction and recognition of their demands. Yet it is clear that this is a highly idealised picture of democratic society: there will in many cases be groups who are not listened to and who are marginalised by the procedures of democratic politics. If democratic politics uses majority rule as the way of taking decisions, there is always the problem of the permanent minority, especially if that minority is defined by its ethnic or racial status. If the minority cannot get 'into the system', or is always denied an equal hearing precisely because of its minority status, then this constitutes an incentive to resort to violence as a means of asserting its identity, or as a public statement (through violent action) that its interests are being overlooked. This has certainly been argued with respect to the recent uprisings in the suburbs of Paris and other French cities in the autumn of 2005 (Donzelot 2006). If groups are excluded, or feel themselves to be excluded, from democratic channels of participation, then violent action may be seen as the most rational means of political action open to them. Even if those channels are formally open and the political system pays lip service to ideals of republican or democratic equality, the opportunities for those from cultural or ethnic or national minorities to actually become representatives and to have any chance of exercising effective participation are limited. Violence may then be the most obvious way of drawing attention to this situation. The danger is that in its turn this provokes an 'equal and opposite' reaction from those holding state power: they then use violence as a means of repressing protest, and once again the aspiration of democratic politics to exclude violence or to make it unnecessary has failed.

The attempt to exclude violence from democratic politics thus runs up against the problem that the democratic state itself, like any other state, employs violence, even though this is intended to be controlled and used only in limited circumstances. Yet the danger is that those charged with using violence to defend democracy may, either intentionally or inadvertently, extend the scope of that violence, with significant consequences for the democratic nature of the order they are supposed to be protecting.

Political violence is thus fostered by the exclusion or marginalisation of groups from the established channels of democratic politics. Democratic systems have always faced a challenge of violence from those who do not accept the legitimacy of the democratic system. In the days of the Third French Republic, for example, nationalist radical right movements like Boulangism attempted the overthrow of the republican system. So too did fascist groups in France in the period after the First World War, most notably in the riots of 6 February 1934 in a direct assault on the Chamber of Deputies. The main challenges to democratic politics in the period of the nineteenth and early twentieth centuries were from movements which were *backward looking*, which sought to reverse the march forward to democracy and the realisation of popular sovereignty. This includes movements like fascism which used some of the tools or appearances of democratic politics (mass rallies, mass propaganda, populist and demagogic discourse) for the very purpose of overthrowing democracy. The situation now is different since the challenge of violence has assumed new forms and arises out of different causes. Identifying these causes and forms has thus become an important task of social science.

The three headings of *nationalism*, *religion* and *social deprivation* function well as signals to indicate the central themes of violent politics in the contemporary world. The movements arising out of these themes do not always challenge democracy as such, as did opposition movements in the past, but in many cases seek a place within it, or challenge democratic politics for not giving them sufficient recognition or for denying their identity and value. Challenges of violence in contemporary politics are therefore frequently an expression of anger (Sloterdijk 2006), directed against democratic institutions with their symbols and processes which proclaim universal messages of inclusion yet do not live up to the aspiration to provide genuine inclusion and adequate recognition of the particular identities of certain sections of the citizen body. While neither nationalism nor religion, still less social deprivation, are newcomers to the political scene, the contemporary world is a more violent one because there is a conflict between a more controlling and potentially repressive state on the one hand and those bearers of identities and values who feel marginalised and affronted by this more concentrated state power on the other. There is thus a contradiction in contemporary liberal-democracies, identified several years ago in very general terms by Andrew Gamble as the opposition between 'the free economy and the strong state' (Gamble 1994). In a neo-liberal economic system the protective role of the state is reduced, with the consequence that the state is less able to secure the conditions for social cohesion. At the same time it attempts to give freer rein to the flow of market forces. This leads to a marginalisation of those who have not profited significantly from the globalised economy of the contemporary world. Yet the category of those marginalised in this way includes more than just those who are the losers in economic terms. It encompasses those who are losers in terms of recognition and respect, who are seen as subordinate, and who feel their subaltern position reinforced by the rhetoric of a 'war against terrorism' which often seems to be a 'war' to secure the hegemonic position of the United States. Violence is spread by the dominant powers at the same time that they claim to be opposing such violence, since in combating terrorism by coercive means they in turn stimulate violence as a counter-response.

In turn this opens up the whole problem of state-sponsored violence, used both by non-democratic regimes as a means of maintaining themselves in power, as well as by liberal-democratic governments who may also be agents of violence. Like their challengers, the holders of state power are equally prone to employ violence, both internally and in an international or global context. State agents in liberal-democratic systems, despite their democratic principles, are in many cases far from reluctant to resort to violence to defend the existing structures of power. In this respect the supposed incompatibility of democracy and violence is far from being a reality.

This then raises the question of how democratic states should respond to the challenge of violence. In what ways and by what agencies can violent politics be 'redirected' so that it takes up the path of democratic politics, defined above as the pursuit of a dialogue in which all can participate, with a hoped-for result of some compromise and peaceful reconciliation of conflicting positions? There are two implications here for the politics of liberal-democracy: the first is the need for the creation of new institutions which are more inclusive than the present institutions of liberal-democracy. At present, the pathways into these representative institutions are quite narrow, in the sense that (for instance) parliamentary institutions (especially in Britain) seem dominated by those coming from a limited section of society. This suggests the need not only for an opening up of existing institutions of parliamentary democracy to a range of people coming from a wider range of society, but also for the creation of new institutions which would facilitate participation at various levels on the part of those who have neither the time nor inclination to devote themselves full-time to a political career (Schwarzmantel 2003). Thus the response to violence in liberal-democratic societies seems to demand *institutional reform*, so that as political structures become more inclusive, recourse to violent means of political action becomes less compelling.

The second implication is that there needs to be a *change in the discourse of politics* – from one that is confrontational and dogmatic to one that puts greater emphasis on dialogue and communication. This is certainly not intended to suggest that a mere change of tone by political elites will have instantaneous or 'magic' effects. But it is to claim that, in place of the rhetoric of antagonism and opposition, it is necessary to develop a new language of politics, one which seeks to highlight the importance of democratic debate and communication (Schwarzmantel 2007), and extending the latter to those who have so far had little opportunity for such interaction. Complementing the institutional reform just mentioned, this linguistic or 'discursive reform' would thus again extend the scope of political debate to those currently excluded from it.

None of this, however, means that a democratic state would ever be able to reach that 'perfect state' of exclusion of all violence that is the ideal of a democratic polity. Democracy is bound in this respect as in others to remain imperfect, since it would still have to employ violence or the threat of violence against those unwilling to engage in democratic politics, even with the extension of opportunities to do so. The crucial implication here is that there must be restrictions and controls on the use of violence, and a greater awareness of the tendency of agents of the state to broaden the criteria under which such violence would be permissible. This too has consequences for institutional reform, requiring breaking away from traditions of secrecy which give more autonomy to leaders of democratic states and in particular to certain branches of the state apparatus who use their power to engage in violence, thus provoking an equal and opposite reaction of violence in turn. The aspiration of democratic societies to exclude or minimise the use of violence as a political weapon is in tension with the necessary employment of violence by the democratic state. The examination of these questions thus requires us to understand the nature and causes of political violence in contemporary politics, and to provide a 'sociology of violence' to explain what is new or specific in the phenomenon of violence today. The hope is that by explaining these issues fully, some conclusions can be drawn concerning the ways in which the challenge of violence should be met by contemporary liberal-democratic societies. The ultimate purpose of such analysis is to suggest appropriate policies and strategies of political inclusion and institutional reform, such that the citizens of liberal-democratic societies might enjoy a greater degree of stability and enhanced freedom to develop their capacities which is the promise of democracy as a way of life.

Political violence is a perennial problem, and historically the attempt has been made to tame it through the power of the state. Democratic politics and the capture of democratic rights were often brought about through the use or threat of violence by those denied such rights, and hence excluded from processes of democratic deliberation. The promise of democracy has been to reduce violence by ensuring that all voices count in the process of democratic reconciliation of conflicts and different interests. The analysis that follows seeks to explain further how democracy itself, while holding a possible key to taming violence by incorporating all voices in a democratic community, can also exacerbate violence, given the transformed and more difficult conditions of contemporary democratic rule. The next chapter therefore seeks to deepen the analysis of political violence in the contemporary world by focusing on the issues of how democracy itself can foster violence, and what can be done to avert this danger. The problem is that challenges to democracy arising from the three factors specified above – nationalism, religion, social exclusion – can provoke a reaction of violence on the part of the democratic state and its agents. This reaction risks inflating executive power and more generally undermining those democratic rights and processes which are fundamental for the whole democratic order itself. The danger is then one of a vicious circle, in which violent challenges provoke similar responses which themselves make more difficult the democratic or inclusive answer that alone might offer a hope of containing or taming the challenges of violent politics. Democracy can thus be seen to be at one and the same time both the problem and the solution, the former if it is interpreted in certain ways, the latter if it were to be transformed in its discourse and in its institutions. It is also problematic in that the attempt to impose democracy as a universal solution to all problems has been identified with great-power interests, and the methods used have gone hand in hand with great-power violence. This raises questions concerning the spread of democracy, to be discussed in Chapter 6 below.

2 The Forms and Nature of Political Violence

The first chapter presented an overview of the issues to be debated in this book. The theme to be pursued further here concerns the nature and causes of political violence, and the ways in which political violence in contemporary politics differs, if it differs at all, from earlier times. It is clear that political violence in general is not a new phenomenon. Indeed, if the argument of the previous chapter is correct, the state itself exists to deal with this perennial problem of political violence. The state as an institution seeks to achieve a monopoly of the use of violence so that members of the society in question can enjoy a degree of security, free from the random attacks and consequent insecurities which would characterise a Hobbesian 'state of nature'. As Locke pointed out, this raises the problem that the state itself could be an agent of insecurity and of violence, so that the remedy might be worse than the disease (Locke, 1988 [1690]). The agents of the state who are entrusted with minimising and containing violence may themselves perpetrate acts of violence against those they see as opposing the existing order. As one recent account of state violence in Latin America makes clear, speaking of the so-called Operation Condor: 'Its larger targets were rebellious sectors of society and popular movements demanding democratic or social change' (Menjivar and Rodríguez 2005: 36). In fighting or opposing violence the state itself uses the same weapons of violence, and this entails a strengthening of the executive and non-accountable elements of the state apparatus. We thus have to consider both the factual descriptive question of how contemporary liberal-democratic states do in reality respond to the challenges of those using violence or the threat of violence, and also the normative theoretical question of how those in power should respond. But before discussing the state response, the nature of violence in contemporary politics has to be analysed. What exactly is the nature of violence as a challenge to democratic politics in the contemporary world?

In this formulation, there is a binary opposition between 'democracy' on the one hand, and 'violence' on the other. This needs questioning, not least because raising the issue in this way risks acceptance of false terms of debate, as they are presented uncritically by those in power. Such misleading terms of debate present 'democracy' in its existing form on the one hand, with 'violence' as challenging and opposing democracy on the other. This is confusing on both sides of the equation, because violence has historically been exercised in favour of democracy, as seeking to extend democracy to groups and movements hitherto excluded from the rights of citizenship. Similarly, those opposing violence in the name of democracy often do so out of a desire to preserve an existing power structure which restricts citizenship rights to a narrow section of the population. It is thus wrong to see violence as necessarily opposed to or challenging democracy and democratic ideals, since political violence is often the response, perhaps an unwilling one, of those who are forcibly prevented from peaceful participation in the processes of democratic politics.

It is thus important to keep in mind the distinction between movements that use violence as a weapon seeking to overthrow democratic structures and processes, and those movements employing violence to extend democracy and to seek entry into the democratic system. Fascist movements in the past and in contemporary situations use violence in an attempt to overthrow democracy. Urban riots and demonstrations such as those that occurred in France in 2005 could be seen not as seeking to overthrow a democratic system but as drawing attention to its defects, demanding that a proper voice be given to those disfavoured and not given sufficient respect by the system as presently operating.

In this way a blanket use of the term 'violence' may not be very helpful, since it is often used with pejorative intent to discredit those engaging in actions that can be described as violent. By the same token, the distinction between violence 'for' and violence 'against' democracy needs to be kept in mind, since violent means can be used with very different ends in view.

The purpose of the present chapter is thus to make more precise the nature and causes of violence in contemporary politics, with special reference to the context of established liberal-democratic regimes. If, as maintained already, violence is not a new phenomenon in relation to democratic politics, or to politics in general, then is there anything distinctive about the forms that political violence takes in the contemporary world? In the previous chapter the theoretical framework presented was one of conflict and community: the argument was that community is needed for a democratic society, but that conflict and disagreement are healthy phenomena, an inevitable element of any diverse and complex society. The issue to be faced is whether such conflict can be contained within the institutions and processes of democratic debate and compromise, settled by rules accepted by all actors in the political process, or whether such conflict inevitably substitutes force for discussion. The questions to be posed concern the causes and nature of contemporary violence, and the extent to which political violence has taken on new forms, compared to earlier forms of violent politics.

Nature of the Challenge

There is something different in the context of contemporary politics, relative to earlier periods in the history of liberal-democracy. As already noted, the discussion here focuses on established liberal-democratic societies, as opposed to those in which democracy is yet to be firmly established. The nature of the challenge which violence represents to democracy can be simplistically understood as involving a refusal to accept the norms of compromise and democratic discussion, and an acceptance of the use of physical force as a weapon to achieve political ends. The question to be probed is whether in the contemporary period political violence is used in new ways, for different ends, and whether the present 'conjuncture' is both qualitatively and quantitatively different in its use of violence. Much political discussion, especially that propounded by official sources in various liberal-democratic systems, presents a picture of a different era of politics in which violence occurs more extensively and with greater danger for the citizens of contemporary democracies. Hence the conclusion is drawn that the power of the state has to be strengthened in order to contain this new challenge, which is presented as being more menacing than were threats of political violence in the past.

As we have seen, political violence in relationship to democratic politics takes diverse forms. Historically, the threat of violence was used as a means of putting pressure on power-holders in order to capture political rights which could not be achieved in any other way. Violence was a tool used by revolutionary movements, where the masses demanded entry into politics and claimed democratic rights which the power-holders were not willing to concede. On such a mass scale, violence could develop in intensified and unchecked ways, a fact noticed by both conservative opponents as well as radical supporters of revolutionary politics. The French and Russian Revolutions provide classic examples. While Edmund Burke in his *Reflections on the Revolution in France* lamented the uncontrolled power of the mob, which he notoriously referred to as a 'swinish multitude' (Burke 1968 [1790]), this was not so different from the regret expressed by the revolutionary Babeuf, in his personal witness to the violence of the French Revolution. Writing to his wife on 25 July 1789, Babeuf described the anger of the people following the storming of the Bastille, that symbol of the oppression of the *ancien régime*. He described how Foulon, successor to Necker as a minister of the king, had been hanged along with his son-in-law and his body dragged through the streets of Paris to the joy of the spectators. Babeuf wrote to his wife: 'how this joy made me ill . . . I understand that the people are carrying out their justice, I approve that justice when it is realised by the annihilation of those who are guilty, but does such justice today have to be cruel?' He reflected how the brutal punishments of the *ancien régime*, the tortures and executions which had 'multiplied everywhere', had inculcated cruelty and violence in the people: 'The rulers, instead of policing us, have made us barbarians, because they are barbarous themselves. They are reaping and will reap what they have sown . . . we are only at the beginning' (Babeuf 1976: 102).

Such a reflection is illuminating for several reasons. It provides a vivid eye-witness account of mob violence, and of such violence getting out of hand. It also contains a profound reflection on the cruelty exemplified in such violence, a cruelty in which the masses had been schooled by their masters under the old regime. Political violence was thus an aspect of revolutionary politics, in which the masses were seeking or claiming their political rights. Because of the way they had been disciplined by the old order, this assertion of political rights found expression in cruelty and violence; anger and passion became the guiding forces in political action intended to take revenge for the repression and brutality of the old order. A similar phenomenon can be observed in the Russian Revolution, involving as it did spontaneous actions directed at those who were seen as symbols of an old order which had practised systematic cruelty and violence to keep itself in being (Figes 1996). The historical record contains many such instances of violence as a mass phenomenon spreading by force of example, as part of a revolutionary process in which the people assert themselves as political actors and express their hatred for an order which has oppressed them and reduced them to a totally subordinate position.

Violence has also been used by holders of state power to oppose those whose aim it was to widen inclusion in democratic society and to extend the scope of democracy from the political to the social sphere. This can be labelled as the violence of the Right, exemplified in military coups, as well as by fascist and authoritarian movements which used violence to come to power and then to destroy the rights and liberties associated with liberal-democratic politics. The brutal repression of the Pinochet regime in Chile was an example of such unrestrained state violence, in which those who had sought to use the previous Allende regime to achieve a greater degree of social equality and inclusion were tortured and murdered in order to safeguard the existing structures of power. Fascism in both theory and practice exalted violence, which its theoreticians saw as an inevitable part of the human condition, hence justifying its practice by the state as necessary. Fascist movements practised violence, as exemplified by the Italian *squadristi*. Italian fascists wished to continue the combat which they had witnessed in war. The idea of the 'trenchocracy' exalted the comradeship of the trenches, the sense of friend and foe which Schmitt was to see as an inevitable part of the concept of the political (Slomp 2009). Thus violence has never been absent from democratic politics. It has been employed by movements as an instrument to assert democratic rights, as well as being used for anti-democratic purposes to overthrow democratic systems or to defend social orders of privilege and to repress movements of change 'from below'.

The question, then, is whether the problem of democracy and violence has assumed new forms, and if so what impact this has had on the working of democratic institutions. New forms of violence have indeed developed in contemporary politics, which have led to changes in the working of the democratic state which profoundly affect the nature of contemporary democracy. The earlier challenges of revolutionary violence came from mass movements aimed at the overthrow of pre-democratic 'old regimes', asserting the right of the masses to take their place within the political order. Violence in contemporary politics is different. It is more concerned with ideas of recognition and inclusion and takes forms which are at the same time both more fragmentary and more global. It is carried out by a much more diverse set of movements seeking inclusion in and recognition by the democratic order. The recourse to violence is fuelled by exclusion, which gives rise to a challenge for the democratic state to respond to these demands for recognition. However, the actual response in practice has often been one of fear, such that political action in existing liberal-democratic societies has often only exacerbated rather than mitigated the challenge of violence.

The new forms of violence involve demands for recognition and inclusion presented by new political agents, different from those mass movements of earlier periods. One key feature of these new movements is their cultural character, their primary concern with questions of belief and identity. The case of Basque terrorism is one example of this, showing as it does the power of nationalism as one motivation for a movement of violent politics. The concession of autonomy in 1979 reduced the appeal of such politics – even if it did not end completely the recourse to political violence – and made it possible for a process of nation-building to take place (Mees 2003).

Violence in contemporary politics thus takes on new forms: instead of mass movements seeking to install democracy and claim democratic rights or overthrow the democratic system, the challenge of violence now emerges from more particular and fragmented groups. Political violence is carried out by smaller groups, whose power and danger may be in inverse proportion to their size, and who have more specific aims. These are not so much for the installation or overthrow of a system of power, as for recognition and acceptance on equal terms with other citizens. Liberal-democratic politics thus finds itself in a sense on a transformed terrain or in a different context, since what is at stake is the development of a more inclusive polity, made more difficult in the absence of the shared identity which marked earlier forms of democratic politics. The solidarity of the nation-state was better able to socialise its members into a common culture, propped up by a shared educational system and common historical memories. While those who announce the death of the nation-state may be premature in this diagnosis, it is true that the nation-state is less effective in this process of common socialisation than it once was. Hence there arises the difficulty of achieving democratic community in the context of contemporary politics, where fewer shared historical memories and integrating institutions are available to bind citizens together in a political community.

Violence arises when groups (or individuals) have the perception that their particular identity and culture are not recognised or given sufficient value in the political unit of which they are part. This may be compounded by social inequality and exclusion, which underpin and exaggerate the sense of not being a part of the society in the fullest sense. Such an analysis does not, however, apply to all forms of violence in the contemporary world: the ongoing fighting between drug cartels and the state in parts of Mexico, for instance, does not stem from lack of recognition or demands for identity on the part of the drug cartels. Nevertheless, one crucial challenge to the liberal-democratic state stems from its failure to achieve a fully inclusive community. This is why the concept of a 'war on terror' is ill-suited to developing an effective response to the challenges of political violence. Other perspectives of democratic theory may offer more effective avenues to explore. The violence which has developed as a threat to contemporary liberal-democracy takes such explosive forms because it emerges from feelings of humiliation, lack of dignity and respect, because it relates to individual and group identities which have not been recognised.

While the concepts of nationalism, religion and social deprivation are good signposts to indicate these new forms of violence, it is evident that none of these factors are themselves new: religion and social deprivation or social inequality have been present as motivating factors for political action in all societies. Nationalism may be more modern and less 'perennial' than the other two factors, although this claim is itself a subject of keen debate among scholars, some of whom argue against the 'modernity' of nations (Roshwald 2006). Yet there can be agreement that none of the three factors are newcomers on the political scene. Why then do they give rise to political violence in new ways which in some cases threaten to undermine the bases of the liberal-democratic order? Conflicts arising from these three factors pose potent challenges to the goals of a democratic polity, defined as a community of those who resort to argument, compromise and peaceful reconciliation of conflict as opposed to violence. The basis of the problem stems from the contradiction between the need for community and the greater difficulty in achieving it which characterises the politics of the present day. A democratic community can only be achieved on the basis of the mutual respect, recognition and acceptance of all its members. Since, as already recognised by de Tocqueville (de Tocqueville 1968), equality of conditions is the dominant norm of the modern world, a democratic community can only be stable and self-sustaining if such mutual respect is forthcoming. Such a community of mutual respect comes up against the problem of greater heterogeneity and difference, where the desideratum of solidarity is harder to achieve. This gives rise to mutual fear and antagonism, where members of particular groups feel they are not valued sufficiently, or where they are not integrated adequately into the full scope of citizenship, often restricted to members of the dominant culture. Hence the problem of violence in the contemporary political system becomes more intractable, since it has taken on new forms which are not so much concerned with overthrowing or installing democracy as a political system, but rather with achieving the full inclusion of a range of very diverse groups in a working democratic system.

Such violence stems from a sense of wounded dignity and a lack of recognition of what is fundamental to individuals and their sense of who they are: this is why these conflicts are different from those of the past. Concerns of dignity and respect were indeed also present in earlier political conflicts, but they are more salient in contemporary politics because of the greater proximity to each other of individuals with different identities, and the greater prominence of demands for recognition. Whereas it used to be the case that ideas of assimilation into a dominant culture were more easily accepted, this is no longer the case. Each individual or group demands rights of recognition and respect as well as a corresponding degree of socio-economic equality to give concrete expression to those rights. Violence has less directly economic aspects, but is more the expression of a sentiment that the fundamental recognition of the person has been violated, resulting in explosions of hostility against the political system and its agents which refuse that recognition.

The Resort to Violence

The recourse to violence is all the more probable to the extent that channels and institutions for the reconciliation of difference are either absent or not available to those who feel that their interests, identity or culture have been neglected or marginalised. The optimistic corollary suggests the possibility of solutions to divert or re-direct the politics of violence into the channels of peaceful democratic politics. Faced with groups and individuals for whom violence is an end in itself, or who find personal satisfaction in violent action, a political way out of the situation seems improbable. Yet in many cases the recourse to violence occurs as a way of drawing attention to grievances or failure to recognise core values of the aggrieved groups or individuals. If the political system fails to provide at the very least encouragement to participate in and engage with its central institutions, then the politics of violence may come to seem, and in fact to be in reality, the only way in which respect, recognition and the valuing of interests of excluded groups can be achieved. This suggests both a 'pessimistic' and an 'optimistic' analysis of the new types of violence under discussion; pessimistic in that issues of culture and identity may be less amenable to the compromise and reconciliation which is fundamental to the processes of democratic politics. On the other hand, it is optimistic in the sense that it proposes a politics of institutional reform that might be able to steer violent political movements into channels of democracy, on the assumption that exclusion can be overcome. The example mentioned above of the violence of Basque nationalism could provide a case to illustrate this: after the Franco dictatorship, the granting of autonomy to the Basque region provided both recognition of the distinct Basque culture and the need for it to have political expression. It also created opportunities for redress of grievances and for those seeking to extend the sphere of nationalist influence. As Ludger Mees points out, 'the institutionalisation of post-Francoist democracy in the Basque country was accompanied by the evolution of a new, historically unprecedented cycle of nationalist power' (Mees 2003: 45). In this case institutional reform contributed to diminishing the appeal of violence. This does not mean that the availability of institutional channels will necessarily and automatically guarantee the absence of violence. However, if violence is in many cases the expression of lack of recognition due to the absence of channels of expression for identity and culture, then the transformation of political institutions to achieve a greater degree of representation and inclusion could help make violence less appealing to those who would otherwise resort to it.

This analysis will provoke dissent from those who point to movements like Al Qaeda, with their expressed wish to do away with the whole structure of western liberal-democracy, which is seen as secular and decadent, and worthy only of destruction. However, while the wish to overthrow the whole democratic system is a central part of the ideology of this organisation, the support it receives would diminish if the institutions of the liberal-democratic order were better endowed with representative institutions in which the identities and cultures of (potential) supporters of Al Qaeda were given greater representation and recognition. The recourse to violence is had by groups and individuals who are not for the most part intent on destroying or overthrowing the liberal-democratic system, even if such an aim might form part of their rhetoric. Violent actions are made more likely when established channels of democratic politics are slanted in ways that make the involvement of particular cultural groups more difficult, or even impossible. The problem, however, may provide its own potential remedy, which lies in the radical restructuring of the institutional framework of liberal-democracy and the provision of different institutions to respond to demands for the recognition and valuing of marginalised identities, hence reducing the need for recourse to violence as the only means of political expression.

Globalisation and Violence

There is one further feature or characteristic which differentiates contemporary violence from that practised in the past. Contemporary violence is new both in form (fragmented movements rather than mass-based anti-system movements) and in content (concerned with demands for respect and recognition rather than with rejection of the political system as a whole). The further feature or difference is the global context of contemporary violence, itself a reflection of novel tools of technology and the ease of international or global communication. The requirements of democratic community are more problematic and difficult of achievement in contemporary conditions. But the challenge has become more global, thus transforming the context in which violence and the politics of violence occur. Political violence directed against liberal-democratic politics has changed its nature, since it is now primarily focused on demands for the transformation of liberal-democracy. This involves the integration of different cultures and groups into the framework of liberal-democratic institutions. But the context is different in so far as these challenges can no longer be dealt with inside the framework of the nation-state – though this is not to argue that nation-states have no role or are 'toothless' in reacting to violence.

The challenge of violence is different not just in terms of the actors involved, but because the actors or agents operate in a global context, one in which there is an imitation effect. In his recent study *Fear of Small Numbers*, the sociologist Arjun Appadurai suggests that globalisation has exacerbated the condition of large-scale violence. The events of 9/11 symbolised a movement to a new kind of war, a transition from what he calls the 'vertebrate system' of the nation-state to a 'cellular system' of a network society, spanning nation-states and fostering a new kind of movements. Appadurai offers some insightful ideas to the effect that in an age of globalisation the nation-state is unable to live up to the classical nationalist ideal of ethnic purity and a community of all those sharing a common culture. This is only one form of the national or nationalist ideal, but it has undoubtedly been a powerful one. In Appadurai's words, 'the nation-state has been steadily reduced to the fiction of its ethnos as the last cultural resource over which it may exercise full dominion' (Appadurai 2006: 23). Because of the development of globalisation the powers of the nation-state have diminished. This is especially true of its economic power, but it applies more generally to its capacity to establish a community of citizens sharing a common culture and a strong sense of national identity. Since what could be called the 'traditional' citizens of the nation-state feel insecure as a result of such weakness, this can give rise to violence against immigrants and cultural minorities generally. Appadurai suggests that minorities are perceived as an 'affront' to the majority community's sense of national purity and identity, or, as he says, 'minorities in a globalising world are a constant reminder of the incompleteness of national purity' (Appadurai 2006: 84), so that globalisation brings with it a greater propensity to violence.

Globalisation has thus shaken up the security once provided, even if in always incomplete form, by the nation-state. The insecurity of what Appadurai calls a 'cellular world' operating outside the existing frameworks of sovereignty and territoriality finds expression in the anger of groups fearful of newcomers, of ethnic and cultural minorities who seem to undermine the cohesion of the nation. In reality of course the security of the nation has long been undermined by economic forces and the spread of neoliberalism, but immigrant groups and cultural minorities provide a scapegoat for the insecurity and anger felt by those groups that have lost out in this new globalised world. Appadurai suggests that 'violence can create a macabre form of certainty', in which anger seeks to annihilate difference and restore a mythical purity. Such an analysis explains the rise of extreme right-wing movements using nationalism as a rallying cry to build up support and seeking to secure the identity of the dominant ethnic group in a 'predatory' way, i.e. by attacking or violently denouncing the existence or legitimacy of other cultures and groups. The relative success of right-wing groups is an expression of the politics of violence, seeking to foster an idea of national purity and turn this against 'the other', the immigrant, in at least potentially violent ways. So globalisation with its attendant insecurities has made violence more likely. It has contributed to the further destabilisation of the nation-state and the security which it seemed to offer to hitherto dominant cultural and ethnic groups.

There is a further way in which globalisation has changed the conditions and the context of violent politics. It is not just the case that the community provided by the nation-state is a weaker force in a globalised world; the changed nature of the nation-state has also created new movements which use violence as a political weapon. This seems to be the central insight in Philip Bobbitt's book *Terror and Consent*, referred to in the previous chapter. As we have seen, Bobbitt suggests that a change in the very nature of the state, from nation-state to market state, has made violence more likely, and indeed violence of a different type, carried out by new agents. He argues that groups in violent opposition to the state imitate the kind of state they are opposing, and in a sense use its own weapons. Hence the violence of contemporary politics is different, since 'terrorists in the twenty-first century will not be like the national liberation groups of the twentieth century that fought nation states but will instead copy the decentralised, devolved, outsourcing and privatised market state of the twenty-first century' (Bobbitt 2008: 525). This means that violent challenges to contemporary liberal-democratic systems are carried out by movements of a global networked character, themselves reflecting the transformation of the nation-state into a 'market state'; as Bobbitt himself puts it: 'the market state is a principal force in transforming twentieth century, nationalistic terrorism into twenty-first century global, networked terrorism' (Bobbitt 2008: 527). If this account is right, it would seem to shed a critical light on the analysis given above, which stresses the demand of those using violence to be integrated into a community whose institutions deny them access. If the nation-state has turned into a market state – which no longer concerns itself with the security of its citizens but exposes them to the risks of the market – then there would be no community into which those using violence could be integrated, and this analysis would be out-of-date wishful thinking. However, Bobbitt himself says that as part of the 'preclusive strategy' which democracies should wage against terrorist movements, 'greater inclusiveness in the societies of the democracies can inoculate those persons who might otherwise be drawn into terrorist activities' (Bobbitt 2008: 529).

The problem of containing violence or steering it into the channels of democratic politics is thus made more difficult by the networked and global characteristics of contemporary terrorist movements. If these movements are diverse in character and have such a global spread, then it is indeed problematic to promote the kind of politics of integration and recognition advocated here, if only because it is not clear who or what is to be integrated. The nature of the democratic state has changed, bringing with it as a corollary different types of movement which use the freedoms and commodification of all aspects of life that globalisation brings with it for purposes directed against that same globalised liberal-democratic order. The nation-state has become a market state, and the enemy confronting it does not seek integration or acceptance in its institutions. In any case even if oppositional movements did seek such acceptance, the changed nature of the state means that there is no 'house' or receptive structure able to accept them. In a market state we are left to our own devices, and the attempt to create structures of solidarity remains a futile one as long as the enemy is 'global, networked market state terrorism' (Bobbitt 2008: 521). Violence is employed by new agents of this global networked type in ways that have changed the nature of the problem with important implications for the workings of democratic institutions.

A State of Permanent Crisis

The concept of permanent crisis focuses the problem of democracy and violence. A state of permanent crisis is one in which executive power is heightened at the expense of the legislative organs of the state. If democratic politics aims at the substitution of rational discussion for violent physical confrontation, then liberal-democratic politics aims at achieving a balance of power between the different elements of the state in order to check and control state power. The problem here is that of strengthening the executive (including the military) branches of the state such that the state changes its nature. In this case the change is not from nation-state to market state (as Bobbitt proposes) but from a limited or constitutional state to an exceptional state, or a state where the autonomy of the executive and repressive arms of the state is increased. The concept of the exceptional state was developed by Nicos Poulantzas (Poulantzas 1974) to describe the fascist state, in which the representative elements of the liberal-democratic state (especially parliamentary bodies) were destroyed and in which the autonomy of the state was heightened in two ways. The repressive and the order-maintaining elements of the state were given almost total power, while the state itself was freed from any constraint or influence from social groups and classes, with the result that state power was placed in the hands of a group who could, in the words of Marx, subdue all classes beneath the rifle-butt (Marx 1973 [1869]: 236).

The concept of the exceptional state can be used in a less extreme way to suggest a process or a tendency rather than a final condition. Violence leads to a slippage of liberal-democracy to another form of state in which the balance of elements of the state apparatus is changed, and where a climate of fear and tension erodes the confidence and mutual trust which in a healthy democracy ought to exist between citizens. If democracy requires a sufficient degree of community so that conflicts can be reconciled through rational discussion, two conditions are necessary for this process to take place. The first is a set of institutions in which such rational deliberation between citizens and their representatives can take place, with a sufficient degree of legitimacy for those institutions in the broader society. The second requirement relates more to the sphere of civil society and the mentality of members of the political community. There has to be a sufficient degree of 'social capital' in the sense of mutual trust between citizens who respect each other as equal interlocutors in a democratic dialogue. Trust between citizens is eroded if one section of the citizen body, or of those who are citizens-in-waiting, are perceived as even potentially untrustworthy or as being unwilling to enter into democratic debate. If there is lack of trust and solidarity between members of a community then such democratic dialogue cannot continue, since it is eroded by mutual suspicion. There is an example of this in Will Kymlicka and Magda Opalski's survey of Eastern European democracies in relation to the concept of the securitisation of the state (Kymlicka and Opalski 2001). If ethnic minorities are perceived as a problem and as potentially loyal to a homeland state, in other words to a state other than the one in which they reside as citizens, as was the case at one stage with the Hungarian minority in Slovakia, then democratic dialogue becomes impossible. The ethnic minority are regarded as disloyal citizens who do not really wish to be part of the state of which they are legally members. Since they are regarded with suspicion by the dominant majority, the relationship to them becomes not one of democratic dialogue but is perceived as a policing or security problem in which distrust broadens on each side. From the side of the dominant majority, the minority is treated as potentially unreliable and therefore in need of increased surveillance and police supervision. From the point of view of the minority, the way in which they are treated further weakens any resolve on their part to see the state of which they are a member as legitimate and attractive: 'Finding a stable *modus vivendi* with a local national minority is difficult when a kin-state, with its own agenda, claims to speak for the minority' (Kymlicka and Opalski 2001: 66). The problem is a broader one which affects all liberal-democratic societies with cultural differences and different cultural groups. If the degree of trust between citizens is eroded because some are regarded as potential terrorists or ready to resort to violence, then one of the basic conditions for democratic dialogue is absent.

The problem of violence can lead to a rebalancing of the political institutions of a liberal-democratic state, in which its security organs achieve greater freedom of action and are subject to weaker control by its representative and democratic organs. It can further erode the mutual trust and respect necessary for a healthy democracy so that a climate of fear and suspicion prevails over the confidence needed to maintain democratic relations between citizens. The rebalancing of the political institutions of the liberal-democratic state has been theorised by several authors in terms of the 'state of exception', a term derived from Carl Schmitt and taken up by Giorgio Agamben (Schmitt 1996; Agamben 2005). It refers to a state in which the repressive and executive elements have a greater weight than the representative institutions which perform the checking and controlling functions. This heightens the 'decisionist' power, the sovereign power to suspend ordinary laws and act in ways untrammelled by the normal structure of law and constitutional restrictions. According to Schmitt, this power to decide on the 'exception' is part of what sovereignty involves: 'sovereign is he who decides on the state of exception'. In his perspective this leads to an undermining of the value of liberal-democracy. Since the sovereign can in case of necessity suspend the normal operation of liberal limits on power, then the guarantees supposedly offered by the liberal-democratic state are of little worth. Democracy is always provisional and liberal-democracy is a purely formal system that masks the reality of sovereign power which emerges more clearly in situations of crisis. What constitutes a 'crisis' is in turn not an objective fact, but something on which the sovereign leader or power decides, so that here again the facts of leadership and emergency power become salient.

Faced with movements of violence which challenge the state, the liberal-democratic state changes its nature. Executive power is heightened and the liberal-democratic state moves towards an 'exceptional state', in which the power-controlling elements of the state have their ability to check and control power diminished. The perception of risk, or its proclamation by the holders of governmental power, can be used in a self-confirming way:

by focusing on the problem of security and the danger faced by citizens, the holders of state power give legitimacy to their own sphere of independent action and in that way the nature of the state shifts. This leads to what one author calls 'pockets of exceptionalism' (Bigo et al. 2008: 10), in which certain groups are targeted as suspicious and as potential sources of violent terrorism. This erodes further the idea of trust between citizens as well as mutual confidence between citizens and their government, both of which are indications of a secure democracy. The road followed by Western democracies in the aftermath of 9/11 shows the danger of undermining or setting aside the values of respect for the individual which are basic to those democracies. A cleavage emerges, sustained by governments themselves, between those groups benefiting from democratic liberties and those who are targeted as suspicious, subject to 'exceptional practices'. Such 'pockets of exceptionalism' become embedded in the normal practice of liberal-democratic regimes and the danger is that they might 'engender or accelerate a process of self-destruction of representative democracies and undermine their values and their institutions' (Bigo and Walker 2008: 18).

Many of the challenges which violent movements lay down to the contemporary liberal-democratic state are demands for acceptance, recognition and inclusion, arising when normal channels are blocked or are unavailable. This therefore implies the need for new institutions to be developed in liberal-democratic societies. Yet in practice the response of liberal-democratic societies has been rather for moves towards an exceptional state which heightens both executive power and the surveillance of citizens more generally. The problem here is precisely the danger of a new form of state emerging in which security is used as a legitimating ideology to justify a situation in which representative institutions and democratic power suffer from the securitisation of the discourse of politics. The path followed by contemporary liberal-democracies thus runs the risk of taking them in the opposite direction from that in which they need to go.

Sovereign Power

In a democracy citizens should exercise sovereignty collectively. However, the response of those holding state power to the challenge of violence has involved a shift in sovereignty towards a new regime of global counter-terrorism. State power is deployed in more concentrated forms in which more autonomy is given to the professional members of the security apparatus. Such developments involve the threat to use violence as a counter-measure, thus shifting the emphasis from the sphere of politics to the sphere of policing and security. A worst-case scenario is used to create the justification for moves towards an 'exceptional state' in which 'security professionals' are given a more significant role and the need for legal and judicial checks on their power is minimised.

This in turn raises the danger of the erosion of democracy, since the holders of state power shift the realm of the political away from democratic norms of debate and discussion to norms of force and *diktat*. While violence can never be eliminated from politics the aim must be to contain and limit its use, as suggested by Walter Benjamin's description of society emerging from what he calls 'the circle of violence' (Benjamin 1977). In his essay on the critique of force (*Zur Kritik der Gewalt*) Benjamin distinguishes between violence which defends the existing order and that which founds a new order or a new law. The former, he suggests, can be called '*rechtserhaltende Gewalt*', a force which maintains the existing order. The latter he terms '*rechtsetzende Gewalt*', the violence which brings a new political order into existence, such as the violence witnessed by Babeuf which overthrew the *ancien régime* and founded a new political system (Negri 1992). Benjamin argues that there is a need to break out of the cycle of violence and counter-violence, in which the state's use of system-maintaining violence perpetuates this cycle. The perspective he offers is one of an exit from the politics of violence, which he refers to as 'civilising the revolution'. The emphasis on sovereign power and the growing autonomy of the agents of state violence both intensify the problem rather than diminishing the appeal of political violence. The problem is how to avoid the contagion of democracy through violence which encourages the political agents of a democracy to use the same methods as those they oppose. In Benjamin's terminology the force maintaining the existing order, the '*rechtserhaltende Gewalt*', may be effective in repressing those movements that challenge the system, but at a cost of infecting the political system of democracy itself with the use of violence and thereby eroding or undermining the *raison d'être* of the democratic system.

The assertion of the sovereign power of the state increases the possibility of its diverging from democratic norms. It risks making the use of violence permanent, thus perpetuating the cycle of violence which Benjamin analyses in his essay. Such use of state power has also a performative or demonstrative function, as is well brought out in Vivienne Jabri's article on the use of torture and the publicity given to the acts of torture and humiliation used by the American occupying forces in the Iraqi prison of Abu Ghraib (Jabri 2008). These indicated how liberal-democracies risk succumbing to the temptation to cross the limits which have to be observed in order to guarantee the foundational values of democracy (Lazar 2009). Once those limits have been crossed, democratic values give way to the unrestricted use of sovereign power, which runs the risk of using law-maintaining violence as the chief means of defending the liberal-democratic order. This then marginalises alternative responses to the threat of violence. One such alternative would involve a transformation of liberal-democratic institutions and a change in the discourse of democratic politics to develop the mutual toleration and recognition whose denial leads to violence.

The relationship between democracy and violence is thus complex and problematic. Violent movements arise in democratic societies for several reasons, among which the most prominent is the lack of recognition of particular identities and cultures. This is a question much more salient in contemporary democracies which are far less homogeneous than in the past, in part due to the importance of migration and globalisation. If the key decision-making institutions and representative forums do not address the needs of significant sections of the population, this can lead to a danger of greater violence. Minority groups are neglected, while the majority feels the nation-state is no longer giving them the security and recognition they once had, so that on both sides the possibility of democratic dialogue and mutual recognition is diminished.

The situation is made more problematic by globalisation. Movements employing political violence can take a global form and, as Bobbitt has highlighted, may take on the more amorphous networked character of the 'market state' which they oppose and wish to overthrow. The issues on which groups clash touch on nationalism and religion, exacerbated by social deprivation, and it is on those issues that compromise and reconciliation are more difficult to achieve since they are less amenable to a solution of the kind where one 'splits the difference'. Furthermore, the fact that the challenge of violence takes place on a global scale changes its practitioners, with whom any dialogue is more difficult because of their extended scale and looser structure. The nation-state is less able to function as a 'container' or receptive structure to integrate these movements or those sections of them who wish for such integration. Hence the possibility of democratic dialogue becomes more problematic. When the response of the state to the challenge of violence is itself to refuse dialogue and to engage in counter-violence this has a number of consequences. It changes the balance of state power, giving greater salience to the security- and order-maintaining elements of the liberal-democratic state. This is what has been described above in terms of the move towards an exceptional state in which state sovereignty is heightened and executive power reinforced. But as we have seen, this securitisation of the state only perpetuates the cycle of violence and narrows the scope for steering away from violence those movements which challenge the workings of democratic institutions.

Finally, these developments have to be assessed in terms of their effect on the mentality of the citizens who are the supposedly sovereign force in a democratic society. Democracy depends on mutual trust both between citizens and between citizens and the political elite. The contagion of violence erodes this trust in both dimensions. If groups of citizens become objects of suspicion and fear, they themselves react accordingly so that the risk of a self-fulfilling prophecy becomes real. Relations of trust and confidence are eroded between citizens themselves and between them and the state, which acts in more violent ways and treats people no longer as citizens but as potentially dangerous objects of surveillance. The political culture of a state of exception is one in which the values of citizenship, public reason and democratic debate are overridden by attitudes of mutual fear and suspicion.

Liberal-democratic societies are indeed facing challenges from movements of political violence. Instead of institutional transformation and a change in the discourse of politics the response has been one of securitisation and state-conserving violence which risks continuing the cycle of violence and poisoning the springs of democratic politics. It is more difficult than in the past to develop institutions and structures capable of steering such violent challenges into paths of peaceful reconciliation. Nevertheless, this should not rule out discussion of the challenge and of the ways in which the threat might most fruitfully be met.

3 The State and Violence

The State as a Violent Actor

The focus of this chapter is on the state itself as a violent actor, and the problems this raises for democracy in theory and in practice. The core issue emerges from the material presented in earlier chapters, and can be stated as follows. The state exists in order to prevent the unrestricted or illegitimate use of violence by private persons or groups. Its function is to guarantee the security of citizens, and to prevent infringement of their rights by other individuals or groups of individuals. In terms of the analysis offered earlier, state power has the function of ensuring that the conflict and heterogeneity which are a necessary and healthy feature of a democratic society do not exceed certain limits. The problem is how to achieve the containment of conflict within the peaceful institutions and channels of democratic politics. The essential idea is that of steering potentially violent confrontation into a framework of discussion, compromise and rational debate, however idealistic that aim may sound. If Churchill's statement that 'jaw jaw' is better than 'war war' is too simplistic an expression of this idea, it at least conveys the basic aspiration to convert aggression and direct physical confrontation into a process of deliberation which involves all participants in a process of debate and allows for the possibility of rational interlocution.

Those who practise violence use fear and terror as weapons (literally as well as metaphorically) of the political process, and this undermines the possibility of democratic dialogue. It is resorted to primarily by those who are excluded or marginalised from the institutions which make such democratic dialogue possible. The presence of violence in a democratic society, therefore, is a warning sign that all is not well with its political institutions, a 'red light' to suggest that there are groups in the system who feel that their demands and interests are not served by the structure of the democratic institutions in place. Violence can exercise a potentially positive function. If there are groups who feel that they can gain more through violence or physical force, then this may well be a sign of the pathology of the political system in question. It may indicate a legitimacy problem, if certain groups do not see the structure of the political system as reflecting or representing their interests. More broadly, the use of violence as a political weapon often results from a situation in which the whole political structure is seen as illegitimate in the eyes of certain groups.

This point is well made in a recent study of terrorism and the responses to it, whose author notes the diversity of the phenomenon of terrorism, defined by him in the following way: 'terrorism involves heterogeneous violence used or threatened with a political aim' (English 2009: 24). Terrorism and political violence have to be explained using a political framework, as English rightly insists, since violence and terrorism are centrally connected with questions of political power. Above all, 'very many of the settings in which we have to explain terrorist violence are ones which involve profound problems of political illegitimacy', and notably 'the political legitimacy problem associated with nationalist terrorism', where the boundaries of state and nation do not coincide (English 2009: 50). This counts as a central example of the failure to recognise a particular identity and culture, with violence as the result of such lack of recognition. These ideas will be further developed in subsequent chapters, but they raise the question of the role of the state in a democratic or would-be democratic society, in connection with its exercise of violence. The basic idea to be developed here turns on the paradox that while the state is supposed to control and limit the use of violence, it can itself intensify and spread violence by its own actions. The state controls violence through its claimed monopoly of the means of violence. Yet the use of violence to control and limit violence is itself problematic and leads to consequences other than those proclaimed and intended by the liberal-democratic state. These are the dilemmas, both theoretical and at the same time intensely practical, which this chapter seeks to explore further. In what ways can and should a democratic state deal with such problems?

The State: Problem or Solution?

It was Locke in his *Second Treatise of Civil Government* who classically posed the problem that the state, conceived as a remedy for the violence inherent in the 'state of nature', might itself prove to be a new and more dangerous source of uncontrolled power. Criticising those (like Hobbes) who argued for the absolute power of the sovereign, Locke famously wrote: 'This is to think that Men are so foolish that they take care to avoid what Mischiefs may be done them by Pole-Cats, or Foxes, but are content, nay think it Safety, to be devoured by Lions' (Locke 1988 [1690]: 328). The state, in a supposedly democratic society, is that set of institutions which claims the monopoly of the legitimate use of force. It does so to prevent the use of violence by 'private' citizens which would, if uncontrolled, lead to a 'state of nature' or a situation of radical insecurity where people's lives and property would no longer be safe from others. The claim is therefore made that the state functions as a societal policeman, which through its agents makes it impossible for citizens to use violence against each other, or at the very least punishes those who illegitimately use physical force to achieve their ends. It is only agents of the state who are entitled to use violence, because such force is used to maintain the overall peace and security of society. Violence, in the form of the imprisonment, punishment and disciplining of persons, is the sole prerogative of the state, whose aim is to achieve the exclusion of violence from the normal activities of society carried on through consent and peaceful transactions.

From its beginnings, liberal political thought recognised the obvious problem in entrusting agents of the state with the sole legitimate use of violence, since the remedy could be worse than the disease. The development of the centralised state gave rise to a source of power which could be deployed against its own citizens. The history of the twentieth century has shown all too vividly the dangers of unrestricted state power. The remedy for liberal thinkers lay in preventing arbitrary power and checking and controlling the use of violence by the state and its agents. The design of a constitutional state was intended to subject state violence to strict supervision and control, so that it was exercised only to the extent necessary to prevent illegitimate violence in the wider society. To achieve this end, independent institutions of surveillance and control of the executive were needed, expressed in the hallowed ideas of separation of powers and judicial review of the actions of the executive, all of these elements being basic to the liberal-democratic state. Given that state power is such a crucial weapon, and that the monopoly of the means of violence provides agents of the state with fearsome powers over (literally) life and death, the exercise of these powers had to be carried out only to the extent necessary to secure the safety of citizens and their protection from violence at the hands of other citizens. These ideas have gained in importance in the light of contemporary technical advances which have increased the ability of the state to control and survey the lives of its citizens.

Here as in so many other fields the core ideas of liberal political theory were developed for a different age in which the tools of the state were less pervasive and less capable of affecting (for good or ill) the lives of its citizens. The classical liberal view saw state violence as reacting to infringements of the law, as punishing those who had themselves illegitimately taken violence into their own hands. Yet this reactive view of the state does not reflect contemporary realities, or the pressure of a situation in which liberal-democratic states have the task of anticipating and preventing terrorist attacks, so that a proactive response is needed. The traditional liberal view of checks and balances and the control of state agents after the event of their use of violence become more problematic in the light of the move towards an exceptional state. The liberal-democratic state has arrogated to itself, following the attacks against its citizens, a more proactive role in anticipating and preventing violent challenges. This has entailed expanding the role of the state in ways which make the state itself a violent actor, using force to discipline its citizens while at the same time legitimating this process in the name of security and safety.

This proactive use of state power widens the permissible limits of state action. The issue here is well presented by a contemporary social scientist who analyses the ways in which new forms of terrorism have, in his words, 'begun to have major ramifications' on how states are able to aspire to the core ideals which are supposedly foundational for liberal-democratic society (Haubrich 2006: 400). Haubrich sums up these ideas under the four headings of liberty, security, equality and efficiency, and his analysis gives us some useful leads. *Liberty* is indeed the foundational value of liberal-democracy, understood as the right of citizens to lead their lives in whatever ways they see fit, free from state power and from the interference of their fellow citizens. The exercise by the state of the monopoly of violence is justified by the claim that this ensures the *security* of its citizens. The protective role of the state secures its citizens' ability to carry out their projects, whatever they may be, in safety. By the same token, this involves an idea of *equality*, since these rights are enjoyed on equal terms by all citizens of the society concerned, and even by those who are residents but not citizens. These rights should be guaranteed by the state with maximum *efficiency*, so that states are competent in guaranteeing the rights and in maximising the conditions needed to make them effective. The danger is that state action using violence to contain challenges to the state undermines those foundational values on which the liberal-democratic state rests. The state itself and its agents become the problem rather than the solution to the threat of those using violence against it, so that the liberal-democratic state deepens rather than resolves the problem. This goes to the heart of the problem of the liberal-democratic state in its present form, since it raises the question of whether liberal-democratic societies risk imperilling their fundamental values in responding to those who use violence as a political weapon. The following discussion pursues two lines of enquiry: the first is to analyse the role of the state as a violent actor, the second to propose in general terms how liberal-democratic states should themselves use limited violence in order to prevent the conflict inherent in any complex society from generating a more widespread violence. Democracy in its ideal and ultimate form aims at the eradication of violence as a political tool. The aspiration is to render violence unnecessary, through the twin goals of social and political inclusion and the recognition of cultural and national difference, where those form the basis of violent actions. How is this achieved, in practice, and how might these aims be realised more fully and more effectively?

What Criteria Should Guide State Use of Violence?

The theoretical question to be posed concerns the permissible uses and limits of state violence (violence intended to control or limit other violence). In turn this raises the much more practical question of whether in practice liberal-democratic states exceed or transgress those boundaries, how the limits of permissible state action can be maintained, and what mechanisms and forms of control are needed to achieve this end.

There are a number of principles which should guide the use of coercive state action in dealing with violent challenges. The term 'violent challenges' refers here to movements which reject established channels of democratic community and debate, though this leaves open the question of the reasons for such rejection. Groups and individuals resort to violence for very different reasons. These may arise out of a visceral hatred and rejection of democracy as such, as exemplified by those who adhere to an ideology of 'jihadi fundamentalism'. Mary Habeck's exposition of such an ideology makes it clear that what is involved here is a view of democracy as fundamentally illegitimate. Democratic societies see power as stemming from the people, whereas on the fundamentalist view it is only God who can order the world and provide the basis for an ordered society. As Habeck summarises it: 'The entire concept of democracy comes in for special condemnation by jihadis . . . jihadis want nothing to do with "man-made" laws or men legislating according to their own choices and desires . . . Jihadis today have made a critique of democracy the centrepiece of their ideology' (Habeck 2006: 72–3). This refusal to see a democratic system as in any way legitimate certainly distinguishes those who take this view from those who resort to violence as a means of seeking inclusion in a democratic system, demanding a recognition that is denied them. Referring to one particular jihadi group (Hizb al-Tahrir), Habeck writes that 'The group has argued that adopting Western laws and democratic rules is so evil that even if laws identical to those of the shari'a were legislated, the fact that they were adopted in a democratic system would make them wrong and "kufr"' (Habeck 2006: 73). (The term 'kufr' refers to unbelief, or acceptance of false ideas.) It is thus important to underline the distinction we have made already between violence as system-rejecting and violence as a call for inclusion and recognition.

This provides us with the first of three normative principles regulating state action in a liberal-democratic society with respect to those who resort to violence: the need to recognise the different motivations for political violence, and to differentiate between the two broad categories distinguished here. The distinction is between those resorting to violence as irreconcilable opponents of liberal-democracy who see it as fundamentally illegitimate, and those whose recourse to violence is a strategic move undertaken because it is seen as the most effective means of drawing attention to their exclusion or lack of recognition. If many of those who resort to violence do so for the second of these two reasons, transformation in the policies and nature of liberal-democracies could significantly reduce the level of such violence. This does not by itself solve the problem of violence on the part of those who see democracy as fundamentally illegitimate. However, if the number of those resorting to violence for other less fundamental reasons can be reduced, this then at least has the effect of isolating those intransigents who could not in any foreseeable circumstances be brought into the ambit of democratic politics.

The second principle relevant to deciding how liberal-democratic states should respond to violence is a principle of minimalism. The state and its agents are empowered to use violence as a means of political rule: the state acts through coercive means, imprisoning people and thus depriving them of their liberty. Entrusting state actors with the right to use such coercive means is a potentially dangerous course of action, because it places such power in the hands of agents who may misuse it. This misuse of violence could take different forms: it could lead to the stifling of legitimate opposition and dissent, using violence against those who question or criticise the holders of state power. It could lead also to the inappropriate use of coercion, designed not to meet a real danger but to humiliate and terrorise citizens in ways which infringe the aims of liberal-democracy. One of the basic values of a liberal-democratic order concerns the dignity of its members, and the respect for their autonomy and worth as human beings. The idea of what the US constitution calls 'cruel and unusual punishment' refers to the exercise of coercion in ways which fail to respect the humanity of citizens. The principle of minimalism is to be understood here as the idea that force or violence should be employed to the minimal extent necessary to defend the liberal-democratic order; in other words, it is a principle of due proportion. Thus the permissible uses of coercion in a liberal-democratic society are those which are strictly necessary to meet a threat to the institutions and functioning of that society. Only then is violent action justified on the part of the state and the agents acting in its name.

The obvious problem here is that of who decides when such action is necessary. Which persons or institutions are to judge when and to what extent civil liberties can be suspended? Who is to decide when a threat is so exceptional that it justifies the coercive interference with rights of the citizen? Schmitt's statement that 'sovereign is he who decides on the exception' (Schmitt 1996) is often cited in this connection, with the implication that the guarantees of liberal-democracy are in the last resort worthless because they have to be suspended if the need arises. In Schmitt's view, a decision as to whether there is a need for such suspension of civil liberties can never be taken in advance, but has to be declared by a supreme leader or sovereign. In that case the liberal aspiration to control power breaks down of necessity. Many constitutions of liberal-democracies contain a clause giving the head of state the power to decide when such emergency conditions genuinely arise. This is the case, for example, with Article 16 of the constitution of the Fifth French Republic, which allows the President of the Republic to suspend the normal operation of the parliamentary institutions when there is a clear threat to the Republic and to its basic institutions. The dilemma which confronts the leaders of liberal-democratic societies is that meeting a threat of violence with the suspension of representative and democratic institutions involves the risk of undermining or eroding those rights and institutions which are fundamental to liberal-democratic political systems. The danger is that the state itself, in conditions of emergency politics, or what are seen as such, gives greater power to the executive elements in the state. This extends the use of violence so that excessive force is used and the rights which define liberal-democracy are overridden or ignored. The state thus becomes itself a violent actor, employing violence in unrestricted ways which then call forth an equal and opposite reaction from those opposed to the liberal-democratic state. Examples from the US war against terror are obvious cases in point here, as witnessed by the abuses at Guantánamo and Abu Ghraib.

This gives rise to a third and final principle, the principle of democratic control. The problem of violence has to be posed both from the side of non-state violence (those using violence against the state) and from the side of state violence. The challenge of violence against liberal-democracy lies not solely in physical attacks on the security of citizens. The challenge also lies in the danger that in response to non-state or anti-state violence, the agents of the state arrogate to themselves a greater autonomy or freedom of action, justifying this through the need to defend liberal-democracy against a threat to its functions and institutions, with the result that rights which are fundamental to liberal-democratic societies are themselves undermined.

This principle of democratic control thus aims at preventing a violent challenge to the institutions of liberal-democracy from undermining or eroding the bases of the liberal-democratic order itself. Such a principle involves the maintenance of institutions of checks and controls over the holders of state power. Institutions and procedures have to be developed which maintain the accountability of holders of state power. These are all the more important in a conjuncture in which those agents are more proactive against those who appear to threaten the institutions of the state. The traditional liberal idea of checks and controls was developed in a context where investigation could be after the fact, and where the use of emergency powers or direct action by the agents of state power was a highly unusual occurrence. In the conditions of modern politics, however, this situation has changed, since the powers of the state are more concentrated and more effective. The surveillance society gives the state in liberal-democratic societies a greater freedom of action, with a correspondingly greater difficulty in maintaining institutions of checks and controls.

The three principles here enunciated – of distinguishing between forms of violence; of the minimal use of coercion; and of the need for control and transparency – are thus all the more difficult to enforce in an age of the 'securitisation of politics' (Nef and Reitner 2009) where an increasing number of issues are seen as security problems, in relation to which agents of the state are claimed to need greater discretion and autonomy.

Thus, in response to the question as to what are the permissible uses of coercion or violence in a liberal-democratic society, the answer is that violence is only permissible to the extent that it meets a 'clear and present danger', that it can be shown to be within the limits of what is strictly necessary, and that it is controlled by open means of scrutiny, transparent to public opinion. The danger of the forms of exceptional politics and the moves towards an exceptional state is that state action in contemporary liberal-democratic societies will elude such control. The use of violence by the state is extended through the autonomy and freedom of action granted to its agents. The pressures of contemporary politics extend the limits of violent action on the part of the holders of state power. Debates in the US about Guantánamo, and recent debates in Britain about the length of time people can be held in custody without charge, exemplify the issues involved in the push towards greater executive and emergency power. The use of violence by the liberal-democratic state now threatens to be extended in ways which mean that the state itself becomes an actor whose use of violence only deepens the problem. Instead of limiting and containing the use of violence by non-state actors, the danger is that the state provokes and spreads violence in the society in question.

Establishing Democratic Rules of the Game

It follows from what has been said above that the state is an agent not only for maintaining democratic politics but also for policing in both a literal and a metaphorical sense the workings of a democratic society to ensure it remains as open as possible to all voices and interests. Yet the other side of the coin is that in their use of violence to achieve these desirable ends the holders of state power tend to ignore the three normative principles set out above: those of distinguishing motivations of violence, minimalism in the use of violence, and the democratic control of its employment. Faced with actual challenges of violence, the contemporary climate of politics lends itself to a 'securitisation' of political issues, where the latter are all made to seem as if they threaten the whole framework of the liberal-democratic state. The consequences of such 'securitisation' are that demands for inclusion and protests against particular state policies are treated as complaints which contest the whole legitimacy of the liberal-democratic order. This in itself has the result that instead of the debate and discussion which should characterise that order, the holders of state power see opposition not as legitimate criticism but as something which has to be met with force and violent suppression. This in turn creates a cycle of mutually reinforcing hostility, as legitimate opposition is met with violence and therefore turns itself to violence. One example of this would be the civil rights movement in Northern Ireland in 1969, where peaceful demonstrations were met by repressive state action which convinced those demonstrating that it was only through violence that there would be any hope of satisfying their demands. This exemplifies a situation where state action intensified conflict rather than steering violent protest into the channels of democratic politics.

A further reason why violence is problematic in the present conjuncture is that those agents of the state given responsibility for counter-terrorism may have a vested interest in inflating the threat faced by liberal-democratic societies. Even if this is not the case, their demands for autonomy of action may make democratic control of their actions – as demanded by the third of the three principles set out above – more difficult.

The exclusion of particular groups from liberal-democratic societies may be felt in different ways. It can take the form of a lack of recognition, where formal civic equality goes hand in hand with real social discrimination or lack of respect, including the denial of cultural rights and of a space for the practice of a particular cultural identity. National oppression, on the other hand, involves situations where the state enshrines a dominant national or ethnic identity, and where those of different national identities then come to see the state as an alien force which neither respects nor recognises their minority culture or nationality. The state is seen rather as a force which acts to maintain one cultural or national identity over a minority one. Violence thus arises since the minority national group feel that its use is the only way in which their identity can be expressed. Violence is seen both as a means of delegitimising the state which fails to recognise a distinct cultural identity, and as a means of achieving a political system which would give recognition to that identity. There is also an international dimension to such violent protest, in the sense that if the foreign policies of a particular liberal-democracy are seen to promote nationalist oppression or the denial of cultural rights, then this too may spark off violence as a means of protest against the policies of the state in question.

The issue, then, concerns the response of the holders of state power to these various challenges. On the one hand, as we have seen, the response of the liberal-democratic state has led to the securitisation of politics, understood as the reinforcement of the relevant branches of the state apparatus, charged with the task of protecting citizens and preventing threats to their security. This process of securitisation runs a double risk of inflating the power of those sections of the state apparatus, while also undermining basic rights which are foundational to the liberal-democratic order. Liberal rights of privacy and mechanisms of control over state agents are overridden in the name of security, supposedly to preserve those rights which at the same time are being eroded. In the same way, the liberal-democratic state becomes less democratic, since the powers of executive action are heightened, and any degree of democratic control and effective popular involvement is diminished because of the greater degree of autonomy and secrecy granted to the security organs of the state.

The danger is that the use of violence by the state itself only intensifies or encourages similar tactics by those who seek to challenge the state, so that the policies pursued go in the opposite direction to those which would redirect the politics of violence into democratic channels of debate and discussion. The state as violent actor becomes an element in the use of violence as a political weapon, rather than the agent of diminishing and controlling political violence.

There are two broad categories useful as tools to analyse these issues: securitisation on the one hand, and the preservation of democratic rights and liberties on the other. Securitisation of the liberal-democratic state does not necessarily involve an abandonment of policies of scrutiny and control of those agents of the state specialising in security matters, but it sees the security of citizens as the chief goal to which other desirable ends must be subordinate. This position tolerates the overriding of basic liberties of citizens in certain cases, subject to the judgement of those 'specialists in security' who have the role of judging the degree of threat and danger posed to the liberal-democratic state. That judgement in turn should be controlled and checked by the representative organs of the state, but with a large degree of trust in those specialists. The value basis of this position then lies in the priority it gives to ideas of safety and security, and the judgement of those who assess the threat of violence.

This position can be contrasted with a distinct perspective given the label of 'preservation'. This takes as its priority the defence of values foundational and basic to the liberal-democratic state. This is not an absolutist position in the sense of holding that under no circumstances must there be any infringement of the basic rights of the liberal-democratic order. But defenders of such a position do not leave the judgement of these matters to the executive branches of the state, arguing instead that the priority must be given to maintaining the rights fundamental to the liberal-democratic state.

Violence which challenges the liberal-democratic state has one of two broad rationales, following the distinction introduced earlier between system-challenging violence and violence which is a call for recognition and inclusion. The former type of violence, exemplified by the quotes from jihadi advocates given above, challenges the foundations of the liberal-democratic order, seen as fundamentally illegitimate and with which there can be no compromise. From the perspective of such fundamentalism, the democratic (or liberal-democratic) state is not one whose premises or institutions can be accepted, since it is seen as waging war against the Muslim world. Therefore, challenging it through violence is both a means of forcing secular liberal-democratic states to reveal their true face as enemies of Islam, and of demonstrating the refusal of the Muslim world to accept a subordinate position.

It is not, however, the case that religion is the only form that such intransigent violence can take. Radical movements like the Baader-Meinhof group in Germany sought to provoke the liberal-democratic state to reveal what they saw as its true character as a violent and repressive state, not so different from fascism (Aust 1987). In the face of provocation (according to the argument of the terrorists) the liberal-democratic state would shed its liberal mask and show its mailed fist, which in turn would provoke uprising and further opposition from an ever wider range of protest movements and oppositional forces. Violence in both these cases, religious and ultra-leftist, was designed not to seek inclusion in the liberal-democratic state but to force it to reveal its repressive character and stimulate opposition to it.

However, in opposition to such challenges, the excessive use of violence on the part of the state or the acceptance of what is here called the securitisation position goes some way to confirming the analysis of the liberal-democratic state offered by its opponents and stimulates rather than diminishes the risk of the recourse to violence. This is not to say that liberal-democratic states and their agents should not meet attacks on their citizens with adequate defence of citizens' security. However, there has to be a recognition that attempts to extend democracy by violence and foreign imposition stimulate in their turn a violent response, and strengthen the view that liberal-democracy is a mask for policies designed to impose one model of democracy, hiding a covert agenda of Western domination. Similarly, the willingness to override basic democratic rights and liberties and to use force against oppositional movements, can be seen as confirmation of the view which those same violent oppositional movements are seeking to propound, namely that the liberal-democratic state is a cover for a far less tolerant and open set of political institutions, and is far from reluctant to jettison its supposedly foundational values.

State violence beyond the minimum thus has the function, intended or otherwise, of contributing to a climate of violence rather than serving as a model of how such conflict should be diverted into institutional channels where conflict is handled in other ways. With reference to those whose use of violence is a call for recognition and inclusion, the response of the state as a violent actor is again counter-productive if it takes the form advocated by the 'securitisation' position indicated here. Using violence against such movements merely deepens the problem since the state responds to calls for inclusion and recognition by refusing to satisfy such demands. The call for inclusion is met by rejection and repression, which again justifies the view of those undertaking violent action that their demands have no chance of expression through the normal channels of politics, but have to be articulated through forms of direct and violent action. Reacting to protests by anti-globalisation movements by deploying the forces of the state in a violent way, as was done in Genoa and more recently in London (at the G20 summit of 2009), threatens those values and processes which are the *raison d'être* of the liberal-democratic state. Such actions on the part of the state undermine any attempt to break the cycle of violence, to use Benjamin's terminology cited in the previous chapter.

If those who resort to violence do so because they feel no other way is open to them, the response of the liberal-democratic state, rather than reacting with violence of its own, must be to show that this perception of those undertaking violent action is misconceived. This involves developing new institutions and a new discourse of politics which would reduce the attractiveness of violence, and suggest that more gains can be made through democratic processes than through the challenge to the institutions of democratic politics. Violence should not be envisaged as practised only by those challenging the state, whether that state is a liberal-democratic one or a state of a more authoritarian type. The state and those who hold state power are violent actors too. The problem for contemporary liberal-democracies is to understand whether such state-approved violence forms part of the problem, or part of the solution. It can form part of the solution if it is limited to what is necessary to meet a genuine threat. The difficulties raised by this statement come of course from deciding what the 'necessary' measures are, and who is to judge the criteria for such measures. The circumstances of contemporary politics and the 'politics of exception' tend to give a greater role in such decisions to those who are themselves specialists in security. But this is problematic from the point of view of democratic values. The state may be part of the problem if it inculcates a culture of violence and acts in repressive ways which push non-state actors further along the path of violence. One essential factor in deciding whether the state reduces or fosters violence is the degree of democratic control exercised over the means of violence employed.

Democratic Transition

The analysis so far has been on the state and its role in established liberal-democracies, facing challenges from violent non-state movements, divided into those that reject liberal-democracy and those who seek inclusion within it. But what is the role of the state and violence in situations of transition to democracy, and what are the criteria for the use of violence in those situations? Here the issues are different, because it is a question of setting the ground rules and establishing institutions for founding a democratic order. In this case, too, the actions of the state elite are of crucial importance. The state has to take decisive action against those who refuse to accept the democratic rules of the game. At the same time, they have to bring in to the democratic process those hitherto excluded, or repressed by the state action of the previous authoritarian or non-democratic regime. The state has to act or to be prepared to use violence against those unwilling to make the transition to democracy. This of course presupposes that there is an existing and efficient state apparatus able to exercise power effectively, and use the sanction of violence against groups who refuse to accept democratic procedures. The South African case is relevant here, since the transitional regime was indeed prepared to use violence against extreme white supremacist groups who threatened to sabotage the movement away from the apartheid system. The implication here is that an effective state which controls the means of violence is a necessary precondition for a transition to democracy. This is the equivalent, from the side of the state, of violence exercised for and in the name of democracy. Violence can be used by non-state groups in the name of democracy with the purpose of securing democratic rights that have been denied. Similarly, on the part of those who hold state power, violence or the threat to use it can be employed to sustain democracy or indeed bring it into being when directed against those unwilling to abide by the democratic rules.

In these cases violence is used by a transitional state to ease the transition to democracy and establish a framework of democratic rule. Yet the capacity to exercise violence necessary for a state to establish democracy can be misused and extended to create a culture of violence which makes the establishment of democracy less likely. If state power is deployed to maintain the hegemony of one particular ethnic or cultural group and repress those who do not belong to that group, then what is created is no democracy at all, but a system which stimulates the use of violence instead of reducing it. Examples can be drawn from some post-Communist transitions where state power was indeed effective in its use of violence, but was used to maintain a particular clique in power rather than to outlaw enemies of democratic processes in general. The case of Chechnya is an example of those holding state power using the violent means specific to the state in ways which terrorised citizens as well as those journalists seeking to expose the truth (Gilligan 2010). Such state violence perpetuates rather than reduces the use of violence. State terror can stimulate political violence by non-state groups, leading to a cycle of repression and terrorism in which each side justifies its actions by the violence carried out by the other side. This is precisely an escalating process of violence which leads to the breakdown of democracy rather than its consolidation.

The cycle of violence then can only be broken by decisive leadership on the part of those who exercise state power to impose some kind of self-denying ordinance which restricts the use of force by the state to the minimum needed to oppose groups themselves using violence to destabilise the democratic order. Here too the international dimension is relevant, since one element in such a self-limitation stems from international scrutiny of the state in question. However, if the agents of this international scrutiny come either from states which themselves have acted in an undemocratic way or from great-power states with their own agenda of power politics, then such scrutiny is itself suspect since it may well be selective in the targets against which it is exercised. States themselves may be reluctant to open themselves up for international inspection in this way, especially in the area of counter-terrorism and security where secrecy and lack of transparency are held to be essential. Therefore there are difficulties in establishing a move away from a culture of violence to a culture of democratic reconciliation of conflict. In a culture of violence, the holders of state power see their hold on the coercive instruments of state power as a precious asset which can be deployed against all forms of dissent and opposition. State power then becomes unrestrained and those who exercise state violence develop the habit and custom of doing so in unrestricted ways, making it all the more difficult to establish a culture of democratic reconciliation.

The violence which followed the presidential and parliamentary elections of December 2007 in Kenya provides an important illustration of the effects of violence on moves towards democracy and of the 'normalisation of violence' which can occur in conditions when the state's monopoly of violence breaks down. Violence broke out once it was announced that Mwai Kibaki had won the Presidency in a fight against his rival Raila Odinga. The literature on these events suggests that once the state loses its monopoly of the means of violence, violence can become both 'normalised' and 'privatised', with the result that it comes to be seen as an acceptable means of gaining or holding on to political power. In the case of Kenya, violence swept through certain areas of the country after Kibaki's victory was proclaimed. Followers of Odinga and supporters of his Orange Democratic Movement were convinced that the election had been rigged, with the consequent exclusion from the Presidency of Odinga and the disappointment of his supporters that they would be denied the opportunities for political advancement and social gain that control of state power opens up.

However, analysis of the events following the election suggests that the origins of the political violence had been latent for some considerable time. The state under the Presidency of Arap Moi had used violence to repress opposition, and had in some cases actively sponsored gangs in a process of the 'privatisation of violence' which ultimately percolated through society. In that way, as Susanne Mueller puts it, 'the very violence used by the state for its own ends at one time frittered away its future monopoly of legitimate force' (Mueller 2008: 192). Mueller's analysis is of more general application. What happened in Kenya was that violence had been the means used by the holders of state power to keep the gains of power; 'power is sweet', one minister in Moi's cabinet is quoted as saying (Mueller 2008: 189). Rather than using the 'normal' apparatus of state power, the state 'manufactured institutionalised violence outside of the state, both by design and neglect' (Mueller 2008: 187). Such extra-state violence was in part generated by those who held state power in order to support their hold on it, but like the sorcerer's apprentice this extra-state violence took on a life of its own and escaped the control of the centralised state. A situation of privatised extra-state violence ended up threatening the integrity of the state itself. The Kenyan case revealed a situation in which political conflict was not settled by debate and discussion within democratic institutions but was contested through physical force and violence, since there was no trust that the institutions available were in any sense impartial or neutral. Well before the contested elections, in some areas of the country violence was exercised by a gang (the *Mungiki*) functioning as a shadow state, taking over the use of coercive power from the centralised state. Thus the eruption of violence after December 2007 was in some senses to be expected, since violence had already been diffused through the whole of society and was seen as part of the normal process of politics. The state had initially encouraged such a process of normalising violence, with the result that it percolated through society and threatened the state's monopoly of violence. Once violence comes to be seen as a natural or normal means of settling political disputes, it is extremely difficult for the state to control it. The lack of institutions perceived as independent and impartial undermined the credibility of the Kenyan election commission (ECK) which had declared Kibaki's victory. In the striking words of two analysts of Kenyan politics: 'The pervasiveness of political violence and the complete impunity of those who routinely use violence as a political tactic is now one of the most striking features of Kenya's political scene' (Anderson and Lochery 2008: 338).

The implication of these events in Kenya during and after December 2007 goes well beyond this particular example. In the Kenyan case, as two different observers note, 'the absence of viable institutions through which conflict could be resolved encouraged activists and leaders to take their protests to the streets' (Branch and Cheeseman 2008: 20). The Kenyan example shows the state both as a possible solution to the use of political violence but at the same time as the cause of the problem. Processes of democratisation and liberalisation of one-party or authoritarian systems need to have certain prerequisites in place to avert violence being the result of such democratisation: 'basic state capacity, the effective rule of law, and an agreed national identity' are necessary conditions for this (Branch and Cheeseman 2008: 26). As these same authors argue, if such conditions are not met then violence is likely to emerge from 'underlying tensions which the state is powerless to manage' (Branch and Cheeseman 2008: 26). This illustrates well the problem of the state as both (potential) solution and equally as cause of the problem. The state in the Kenyan example exacerbated the use of violence as a political weapon, firstly by using violence to repress opposition and secondly by acquiescing or even encouraging the use of violence by 'unofficial' or extra-state gangs. The consequent normalisation and privatisation of violence undermined the capacity of the state to form part of the solution to the problem. The loss of the state's monopoly of violence meant that social tensions burst out in forms of aggressive conflict. In the Kenyan case, these were ethnic conflicts, or class tensions over land (Anderson and Lochery 2008). They exploded into violence once the disputed results of the December 2007 elections unleashed these conflicts and provided for them to be resolved not through democratic procedures but through violent hostility against what Lynch calls the 'ethnic Other' (Lynch 2008).

State use of violence and patronage of extra-state violence thus reduce the possibility of peaceful reconciliation of conflict. On the contrary, they lead to a situation in which violence becomes the accepted and normal means of pursuing political ends. Worse than that, they involve society in an accelerating process of violence, since citizens have to defend themselves against violence by themselves resorting to such means of political action, in a self-fulfilling process of violent counter-action.

In more general terms, the problem of state use of violence is made all the more difficult because of the increased powers of the state. New technology and new powers of communication and surveillance reinforce both the challenge of violent movements as well as the ability of state power to control its citizens. Broader social considerations also deepen the problem: if a society is divided by ethnic and cultural divisions which undermine a sense of mutual trust between its members who are themselves subject to feelings of insecurity and fear, then it is easier for holders of state power to use such insecurities to justify claims to extensive state surveillance and control. This then only deepens a climate of fear and insecurity, so that another self-perpetuating cycle is created, this time of fear, suspicion and extended state power.

In cases of transitions towards democracy, the danger is of state institutions coming to maintain the power of a ruling group or ethnic clique, so that the democracy instituted is from the beginning flawed and incomplete. The challenge is therefore how to ensure that the state, with its monopoly of the means of violence, becomes a means of reducing rather than promoting violence.

State violence has to be checked and controlled, and exercised only when it is necessary to defend the basic institutions and rights of the particular liberal-democratic order. The use of violence by state authorities has to be subject to defensible criteria of transparency and openness, with necessary distinctions between the types of violence being combated.

Only when political violence has been examined with reference to those state authorities defending the established order as well as from the side of those challenging it, can one discuss how *from both sides* a culture or climate of violence could be transmuted into one of democratic reconciliation and compromise. From the side of those wielding state power the change has to involve the control of their use of violence, and the understanding of the purposes and aims of those wielding violence for political ends. This latter would involve distinguishing between violence as an irreconcilable act of opposition to the liberal-democratic order and violence as an expression of blocked channels and the wish to be included in the ambit of liberal-democracy.

A perspective of 'securitisation' risks turning expressions of discontent and opposition into issues which are presented as challenges to the structure of that system itself, so that demonstrations and protests are met with the heavy hand of state repression. This in turn contributes to the alienation of opposition movements from democratic channels and institutions which ought to be the framework for dealing with the conflict which is a normal part of any complex society. Moving away from a climate of violence to a culture of democracy must involve acceptance of the normality of difference and indeed of conflict. The day of the nation-state with a relatively homogeneous national culture is a thing of the past, and political action now has to take place in a society of far greater diversity. The diverse nature of any given society may lead to violence if the traditional majority is unwilling to accept such diversity and difference and if it uses state action to maintain what is seen as its threatened position. In such a case violence arises on the part of those excluded, who are maintained in an inferior social and economic position. A more positive response to violence, whether practised by the agents of state power or those protesting against it, is for a different discourse of politics to be developed, and for new institutions to be formed which meet the demand for greater inclusion. A new inclusive culture of citizenship has to be developed. Before discussing how that could be achieved, the task of the next chapter is to investigate further the challenge of violence, this time not from the point of view of the state as violent actor, but from the point of view of those using terrorism to oppose the state.

4 Democracy and Terrorism

The aim of this chapter is not to provide new factual information on terrorism in the context of established liberal-democratic societies, but to take further the arguments of the previous chapter by considering in general theoretical terms the nature of the challenge which terrorism presents to such societies. In what ways does terrorism threaten the ideas and institutions of liberal-democracies, and are there any ways in which this challenge could be neutralised so that the use of violence for political ends could be diverted into the framework of democratic structures and the processes of democratic politics? These are the general questions which this chapter seeks to answer.

The Nature of Terrorism: Defining the Phenomenon

The first task is to relate the definition of terrorism to the perspective offered in the opening chapter. It was stated there that conflict in democratic societies is inevitable, and that it stems from the different interests and values that will be held by individuals and groups in any society apart from the simplest and most basic. The problem for democratic societies is how to tame this conflict, so that the divergences can be contained within a common framework of debate and discussion, which permits both compromise and the recognition of difference and of the right to hold divergent views.

Terrorism uses violence and the threat of violence as a political weapon and takes conflict to a new level through the use of specific *means* of conflict and political action. In that way it breaks through the limits of democratic politics. While the question of how to define terrorism has received a wide range of different answers, terrorist movements are defined here in straightforward terms as those movements that use or threaten violence against members of the state apparatus as well as against innocent civilians. Such violence is used for political as opposed to criminal ends or ends of personal enrichment. Terrorism is a fundamentally political phenomenon in that it aims at the transformation of society in the name of some cause or of certain values, which are made explicit through statements and manifestos explaining the cause in the name of which violence is exercised against the targets of state and civilians alike. The definition of the phenomenon is thus related both to the *means* terrorist movements use, i.e. violence against these broad targets, and to the *ends* they seek, which are those set by the political goals of the group in question. Terrorism arises out of one of the fundamental aspects of democracy itself, though this sounds very paradoxical. If democracy is about conflict, terrorist movements are evidently expressions of conflict and disagreement, and they arise out of the very nature of difference inherent in any democratic order. However, where they go beyond the bounds of the democratic order is in the means employed, which are those of violence and intimidation.

This present discussion seeks to investigate what exactly it is about terrorism that challenges the democratic order and how liberal-democracies can and should respond to this threat. If democracy is concerned with the elimination or exclusion of violence from political life, how can it deal with movements which make violence their central means of political action? The first problem is that of the ends which terrorist movements pursue. With respect to movements which use religion as the justification for their use of violence, the political aims cited as the ends to be achieved are both vague and general and clearly incompatible with any recognition of 'difference' and pluralism. The demands of movements like Al Qaeda vary from the more specific to the more general. The former are exemplified by the demand that the United States and its allies should withdraw from Arab countries. The latter maintain that democratic societies and the Western model of secularism are fundamentally evil, so that there can be no tolerance of the democratic way of life with its separation of religion from politics. Such demands evidently reject pluralism and the right of individuals to decide autonomously how they should live. The challenge of terrorism to liberal-democratic societies is therefore not just about the means employed, namely coercive violence directed indiscriminately at the state apparatus and its agents as well as against civilians. It is also about the ends that terrorist movements are seeking to achieve.

Notwithstanding the sheer variety of movements which use terrorist tactics, one can offer a broad typology of two types of terrorism, with consequent implications for the responses that should be developed by both citizens and governments of liberal-democratic societies. In the first place terrorism and political violence in general can arise from a deep hostility to the idea of democracy and all that it is seen to entail. The second broad category is much more specific, and involves the use of violence as a means of seeking inclusion in the institutions of liberal-democratic society, or of employing violence as the means of forcing more specific policy changes. The response of liberal-democratic societies in each case has to be different.

Many discussions of terrorism see it as a problem to be solved by state action using tactics ranging from infiltration of terrorist groups to increased security and scrutiny of citizens' actions. A more fruitful path to understanding the nature of the phenomenon of terrorism must surely be to relate it to the nature of democratic politics. However paradoxical it may sound, terrorism in its modern form is a phenomenon of democratic politics and is related to the mechanisms and nature of that politics in a variety of ways. While terrorism targets members of the state apparatus, one of its characteristics is the wider use of violence against innocent citizens selected as random targets for terrorist actions. Terrorism therefore operates by attacking members of the citizen body as a means of exercising pressure on the whole democratic community to change the politics carried out in its name. By extending their activities to include 'ordinary' citizens as objects of attack, terrorist groups make use of a sense of democratic community with the aim of exploiting sympathy with victims of terrorism and the fear experienced by other citizens as a means of changing policy. If terrorism has to be seen as a rational form of political action rather than as some pathological upsurge, its purposefulness stems from the use of certain tactics as a means of changing public opinion.

Public opinion is clearly a fundamental factor in the politics of a democratic community. The democratic method in its ideal form involves addressing public opinion through means of rational discourse and civic education in the broadest sense, so that informed and self-conscious citizens can debate among themselves and form opinions which are then translated into governmental action. While this is clearly an idealised description of democratic politics, it identifies public opinion and the rationally formed will of a body of citizens as having in normative terms the determining role in democratic politics. It clearly fits in with a theory of democracy derived from Rousseau in which discourse between citizens forms the 'general will' of the citizen body, where the government is the executive agent carrying out such an agreed will once it is formed. While one does not have to agree with Rousseau's very unitary view according to which the general will of the citizen body could tolerate no differences, it is clear that in his perspective it is the consciousness of the citizens, in other words public opinion, that ought to be the factor controlling and determining the policies which should be carried out by the government of a democratic society. Power should emerge from the deliberative processes carried on by all those who are members of the civic association or body of citizens.

In the same way as hypocrisy is the tribute which vice pays to virtue, terrorist groups or movements pay a distorted homage to democracy. They seek in some ways to work through the mechanisms of democratic politics by short-circuiting some of its normal routes. Terrorism as a political tactic aims to influence the supposedly determining factor of popular sovereignty by changing public opinion. The aim of terrorism is to alter governmental policy by influencing the sovereign power, namely the will of the people. It does so by making part of that people the target of its violence, arousing the sympathy of fellow-members of the public for those who have been targeted. The aim is to draw the attention of the public to the issue which has supposedly not been addressed by governments or the state apparatus. Thus terrorism can be seen as a kind of public appeal, not in the democratic sense of engaging in discourse or rational statements of intent, but using violence as a means of addressing public opinion. Such violent acts exploit emotion by arousing both sympathy with the randomly selected victims of terrorism and fear that further terrorist attacks will affect other as yet unaffected sections of the public. They may also seek to draw attention to issues that have so far not been addressed through the normal processes of democratic politics. This is not to claim for terrorism democratic virtues that it does not possess, but it is to say that its *modus operandi* is designed to change public opinion and in that way alter government policies. Terrorist activities make the assumption that in a democratic system it is the force of public opinion that is the determining factor, and hence political action, including violent action, has to focus on the citizen body in order to achieve its ends.

Terrorism can thus be defined as the attempt to influence democratic politics by changing public opinion through the use of violent means. It abandons the path of democratic politics in its methods, which are not those of rational discourse. Terrorism seeks to reach the democratic locus of sovereignty (public opinion), but does so by means distinct from democratic practices of rational discourse and civic education. The justification for their activities offered by movements which use terrorism is that the practices of rational discourse and civic education, working through the established institutions of democratic politics, have failed to address specific issues and have not succeeded in providing the recognition and respect due to all members of the democratic association. Terrorism is thus in some fundamental way an expression of democratic politics and arises in the context of such politics. It does so both in its appeal to citizens as a whole and in its attempt to transform public opinion through the use of violence and the emotions of sympathy and fear it provokes. Violence is justified by the claim that certain issues of policy and recognition have not been addressed, but should have been dealt with given the very premises of democratic theory itself.

This does not mean that political violence as such is a phenomenon limited to liberal-democratic societies, but that modern or contemporary terrorism can only exist in a context where two conditions hold. The first is that it is public opinion or the voice of the people that determines what governments do. The second is that all interests and identities have an equal right to be heard and respected, and that failure to fulfil that right can justify the resort to violent means in order to secure a hearing or a recognition that has been denied. The rather unsettling conclusion to be drawn is that in some senses terrorism is a child of democracy, or a perverted offspring of democratic politics, and that it consequently represents a challenge to democratic politics on its own ground. This has serious implications, to be pursued below, both for the responses to terrorism which are in fact practised by democratic governments and for those policies which ought to be followed.

The ways in which terrorism challenges the ideals and practices of the democratic order differ, since 'terrorism' cannot be treated as a homogeneous or undifferentiated entity. In some cases, it can be understood as a protest against the particular actions or stances of the government of a particular society. Some analyses of the terrorist acts of 7 July 2005 in London suggest that they were a protest against the British government's foreign policy with regard to Israel and Palestine, and with regard to the Muslim world in general. This use of political violence is then seen as an emotional appeal to public opinion intended to draw attention to a set of policies which need to be more widely debated and questioned. Other forms of terrorism arise out of the demand for recognition of a particular national or ethnic identity whose claim to autonomy or self-determination has not been realised in existing institutional or constitutional arrangements. The examples of IRA or Basque terrorism would clearly fit this category. Still other forms of terrorism arise out of an opposition to the idea of democracy in general, seen as an illegitimate and blasphemous form of political rule which arrogates to human sovereignty arrangements and political forms which ought to be referred to the sphere of religion, determined by God's will. Here, evidently, the ends to be achieved through acts of political violence against citizens are not ones which could command, in any conceivable discussion, the assent of the citizens of a democratic order.

If political violence of a terrorist kind is used as a means to an end, the ends of some forms of that violence could only be achieved by the total dissolution of democratic community and democratic forms of politics. By contrast, in some of its forms terrorism calls for changed government policies or for the inclusion and recognition of distinct groups, while other types contest the bases of the democratic order as being themselves fundamentally illegitimate. Meeting the challenge of the first two types of terrorism (calling for policy change or for more recognition) will contribute to marginalising the opposition of those groups who wish to contest the democratic order per se.

Responses to Terrorism

The aim here is to suggest how a democratic community can and should respond to the challenge of terrorist violence. The implication is that liberal-democratic societies have pursued strategies of dealing with such violence which operate with misleading conceptual tools, treating the problem as one of security rather than inclusion. If terrorism is in many, though not all, of its manifestations a demand for inclusion and recognition rather than an all-out assault on the liberal-democratic state, then the appropriate response has to be one of transformation of its institutions and of democratic reform rather than the reinforcement of the security apparatus of the state.

Liberal-democratic governments have seen it as their duty to protect their citizens and to use the apparatus of the state to defuse the threat of terrorism through the means specific to the security agencies, whether the normal police force or specialised agencies dedicated to the task of combating terrorism. However, if we follow the suggestion made above that the first task must be to 'disaggregate' terrorism – in other words, to be aware of the manifold dimensions of the problem and the distinction between different types of terrorist movements – then the response of liberal-democratic societies to the challenge of terrorism has to go beyond seeing it purely as a problem of security and to develop other and broader responses.

Terrorist movements aim to affect public opinion by drawing attention to issues which in their view have been 'swept under the carpet' by the normal operation of liberal-democratic politics. This may occur, as in the case of nationalist terrorism, because such processes of normal operation give power to a majority defined predominantly in national or ethnic terms. A minority cultural or national group is thereby assigned a permanent ineffective minority status and denied any significant degree of autonomy. In other cases, terrorist groups claim that their activity helps to unmask the truth about the liberal-democratic state, revealing its coercive and repressive character which is concealed by the operations of day-to-day politics in which representative bodies (Parliaments) function as a 'fig-leaf' covering the real dictatorial or illegitimate nature of the state. Such arguments were offered by terrorist groups using the language of Marxism, such as the Baader-Meinhof group in Germany or the 'Red Brigades' in Italy and similar movements in other countries, including Britain. In claiming that actions of a terrorist kind would reveal the true character of the state and its agents, their hope was that such a realisation would spread to wider strata of the society and thus stimulate some kind of popular socialist revolution against the existing order. It is clear that terrorist actions thus involve a contradictory logic, given the obviously minority character of the violent action on the one hand, and the aspiration to arouse the majority of the citizen body and stimulate them to sympathy with the minority against the repressive state forces on the other. In this respect twentieth-century terrorism borrowed from earlier movements, in particular from some forms of anarchism which believed in the concept of the '*minorité agissante*' or active minority which would through its bold actions stimulate the wider masses of the labour movement to consciousness and action in opposition to the bourgeois order. In actual fact terrorism has had the opposite effect, whether in its nineteenth-century syndicalist form or in its twentieth-century version. It has tended to provoke only revulsion against the violence inflicted on citizens and thus strengthen rather than weaken the existing order.

Thus rationalisations or justifications of terrorist action have been based on claims of drawing attention to grievances claimed to be insoluble through the normal channels of democratic politics, or on claims to reveal the true face of the bourgeois state through provoking state agents into violent actions which cause revulsion in a broader public. Further examples of terrorist action have to be related to the phenomenon of globalisation and the internationalisation of politics (the subject of Chapter 6), but they too have a kind of 'demonstration effect', intended to draw attention to issues such as the denial of the right to statehood of the Palestinian people, and the claimed offensive of the West against Muslims and against Islam in general. Such were the defences made of the terrorist attacks of September 2001.

Terrorism and the violence which it practises thus represent a particularly forceful challenge to both the ideals of democracy and to its institutions. Terrorists appeal to the conscience of democratic citizens by seeking to reveal what could be called the hidden face of liberal-democratic societies, or seeking by dramatic actions to call attention to injustices perpetrated in the name of democracy. Such actions are justified by the claim that there is no way of publicising these issues other than by acts of violence. Assuming that terrorism is a rational political strategy rather than an action carried out by people who thrive on or who enjoy violence for its own sake, then it can be seen (if one accepts its premises) as a means of arousing the conscience of democratic citizens and forcing a change in public opinion which would not be possible by any other means.

Democratic Reactions to Terrorism

The appropriate response has to be couched within the terms of democratic theory and practice, in other words by countering the arguments of terrorism through an 'equal and opposite' appeal to public opinion, since the latter constitutes the basis of democratic politics. Instead of using a discourse of order and treating terrorism purely as a security issue, the response of governments and citizens of a liberal-democratic society to the challenge of terrorist violence has to be different. It has to meet the threat by showing the falsity of the claim that the particular issues used to justify terrorism can be highlighted only through violent action. But the ways of doing this will vary with the type of terrorism involved and the nature of the particular tactics terrorist groups deploy. Terrorist violence has been used as a way of pointing out the exclusion of a particular group, usually a national or cultural one, from equal participation in the democratic process. If such a group can be incorporated in the democratic process through means of negotiation and democratic dialogue, and if the institutions of the liberal-democratic state can be reconfigured to allow the recognition and the autonomy of the national or cultural group in question, then the justification for terrorist action as the only means of drawing attention to the issue loses its validity.

One could see the process here in terms of two opposed forces both appealing to the 'court' of public opinion. The first force is that of a terrorist group speaking in the name of a particular oppressed or excluded section of the political community. The claim is made that violent action targeting citizens at random is one means, and the only one available, of revealing the oppression or exclusion of this minority group. However, the 'equal and opposing' argument could be effective and deny terrorist groups any justification if it could be shown that there are institutions and processes available, not only to draw attention to the identity and capacity for self-rule of the oppressed group, but beyond that, institutions which permit this identity to be recognised and flourish free from oppression by a dominant culture.

This suggests that terrorism can be seen, if not in a positive light, then rather as a sign that liberal-democracies are not living up to their proclaimed or professed principles. The most effective way of responding to this challenge is to minimise the distance between the principles of liberal-democracy and the reality of the society in question. Terrorism functions as a challenge to liberal-democracy and can be effective only where there is such a gap between principles and reality. As one recent account (Gupta 2008) makes clear, terrorism is carried out by individuals who are associated in a group and who commit acts of violence from a sense of collective identity. Gupta makes it clear that it is not a particular grievance as such which is sufficient on its own to create a terrorist challenge to liberal-democratic society. Gupta's analysis points out the importance of those whom he calls 'political entrepreneurs'. They raise consciousness and awareness of 'historical grievances'. Without such leaders to 'frame' the issues, particular grievances would not be articulated in movements capable of using political violence to draw attention to them. The 'framing' has to be capable of convincing, in the beginning at least, a small number of followers who constitute the nucleus of a movement. Gupta's definition of the sufficient conditions required for collective action of a terrorist (and other) sort is worth quoting: he writes of a 'strong enough *collective identity, which is formed through the framing of a grievance by political entrepreneurs by expressing them in the context of religion, nationalism or economic class*' (Gupta 2008: 73, original emphasis).

Such 'political entrepreneurs' are significant for the 'framing' of grievances in a broader context. However, terrorism and the use of political violence within liberal-democracies only constitute a significant challenge if the dissenting group of those practising terrorism can count on at least the sympathy, if not the wider active engagement, of broader circles of citizens. To be effective they have to appeal to public opinion and make a convincing case that the grievances highlighted by the political entrepreneurs and their immediate following are in reality ones which can only be solved or addressed through the use of violence. An effective response to that challenge would have to involve a convincing attempt to show that what Gupta calls the 'historic grievance' exploited by the 'political entrepreneur' is one which can be addressed through the normal processes and structures of liberal-democratic politics. If that can be shown, it would erode any sympathy for the terrorist movement from a wider public. It would reduce support from members of the group in whose name the exercise of violence is carried out, since alternative methods are at hand for securing a degree of autonomy and recognition.

Terrorism can be a serious challenge to a democratic society only if it goes beyond the actions of a small minority and arouses the sympathy of larger sections of the democratic community. Gupta's analysis can be followed here, with its emphasis on the stages of development of terrorist groups, starting with a historical grievance exploited by 'political entrepreneurs', who are then able to mobilise a group of followers to engage in actions which seek to appeal to a wider section of public opinion. The headings of 'religion, nationalism or economic class' suggest that these three factors function as the bases of political violence by focusing on the 'historic grievances' which Gupta rightly sees as necessary, though not sufficient, causes of terrorist action. The distinction which needs to be made here is that between terrorism as a *policing problem* and terrorism as a wider *political problem* securing at least the passive support of a significant section of the population. If terrorist groups are limited to a restricted circle of activists, this becomes a security problem to which liberal-democracies can respond through the normal institutions whose task it is to guarantee the safety of citizens from harm. This is one of the core roles of the liberal-democratic state, whose primary role is to protect citizens from violence, while at the same time ensuring that they are protected from arbitrary state power.

However, terrorist activity becomes a political problem in the broader sense, extending beyond a narrow band of activists, when its challenge to the liberal-democratic state finds resonance with wider sections of public opinion. This results in a swelling of the ranks of the terrorist organisation, and in a broader sympathy with the aims of its activity. Indeed, it seems doubtful if an organisation which succeeds in securing wider support for its aims and activities could be called terrorist, since (on the definition provided here) terrorism is a minority political strategy using violence in order to arouse and awaken public opinion. Once that task is achieved violence becomes redundant, since the job has been done, and the political organisation in question has succeeded in crossing a threshold towards a political solution of the grievance which was the basis of its activity in the first place. Examples of nationalist terrorist groups such as the IRA and ETA are relevant here as movements whose political entrepreneurs exploited 'historic grievances' and sought to expose the denial of national rights by the larger state (Britain, Spain) within which those nationalities were confined. They used political violence to such an end and in both cases were able to do so because of a wider sympathy in their immediate community for the objectives they sought to achieve, which were ones of national liberation, broadly defined. However, terrorist activity comes up against a certain limit when it is possible to show to a wider public opinion that a given 'historic grievance' and its contemporary political manifestations are *not* neglected by the political community in question. Two consequences then follow: the first is that the suffering inflicted on innocent victims of terrorist activity causes increased revulsion among the wider public, and can no longer be accepted as a necessary cost of drawing attention to past violence inflicted on the community for which the terrorist groups claims to speak. The second consequence is that the claim made that terrorist violence is necessary because no other means are available to resolve the historic grievance becomes increasingly untenable.

Once a wider public opinion in a liberal-democracy becomes aware of the issue that has been previously ignored, and which the terrorist group has brought to its attention, then political violence becomes unnecessary. The implication of this scenario is that public opinion, now aware of the 'historic grievance', would influence the holders of state power to become involved in processes of dialogue and discussion and seek peaceful means of democratic reconciliation of the conflicts involved.

The analysis offered here suggests that terrorism may be a permanent problem in liberal-democracy in the sense that resort to violence will be a constant feature of democratic politics where certain groups can make a plausible claim that this is the only way in which their past and continuing exclusion can be drawn to public attention. Terrorist violence is likely to rise and fall, having some success when a plausible claim can be made that no other means are available. The corollary of this is that when this claim loses plausibility the degree of public sympathy, however covert and implicit, and the willingness of potential activists to join the movement, will both diminish. Terrorism then moves from being what is here called a political problem to a policing problem, to be tackled by the 'normal' apparatus of the liberal-democratic state charged with guaranteeing the security of citizens. The aim then must be to restore an idea of democratic community which would render terrorist violence unnecessary by addressing the issues of religion, nationalism and social deprivation wherever they constitute the bases of terrorist violence.

Restoring Democratic Community

Terrorist violence is thus a symptom of some failure in the democratic community. This, it should be emphasised, does not mean that terrorist violence is morally justified. However, it poses in acute form the urgency of the question highlighted in the opening chapter, that conflict has to be 'steered' from violent confrontation into democratic channels where 'historic grievances' can be addressed through peaceful means. This is not meant to suggest that the threat of terrorist violence could ever be finally or permanently removed from liberal-democratic societies. Nevertheless, what is meant by the restoration of democratic community is the inclusion and recognition of as wide a range of interests and identities as possible, so that the recourse to violence is seen as unappealing by those who might otherwise be tempted towards violent action. In particular, this is aimed at those sections of the citizen body that might be attracted to membership and active support of a terrorist group, and those broader strata that might provide passive support for the use of violence outside democratic channels. Terrorism can only be effective and a serious challenge to democratic politics if it attracts support from those who are tempted to become activists as well as from its passive sympathisers. The challenge of terrorism to democratic politics can therefore only be met if both of these elements (activists and passive supporters) are neutralised, or rather if they are included in the process of democratic politics. In that way the incentives for terrorism and for its justification are removed. But again, this does not necessarily mean that terrorist violence could ever be totally absent from democratic politics.

A policy of democratic inclusion, of what is here called the restoration of democratic community, has the best chance of meeting the challenge of violence. The question of course is how such a restoration of democratic community is to be achieved, and whether it is best understood in terms of a restoration or of a creation. The term 'restoration' implies the bringing back of what existed previously. But what is involved here is not so much the restoration of something that used to be in existence, as the development of a new democratic community which includes groups hitherto uninvolved in the institutions and processes of citizenship.

The challenge of terrorist violence is thus one which requires liberal-democracies in their existing form to change, so that the grievances exploited by the 'political entrepreneurs' of whom Gupta speaks can be handled through non-violent means rather than furnishing the basis for violent actions or for sympathy with those who carry out such actions. The achievement of democratic community involves the integration of alienated groups through a process of recognition and acceptance, leading to the recreation of citizenship to include in the citizen body those hindered by economic and social deprivation from effective participation in its activities.

Violence arises from resentment and feelings of disrespect, with the concomitant realisation of exclusion from the culture of the majority community. Hence the recourse to violence is stimulated by anger, as Sloterdijk suggests (Sloterdijk 2006); in this case a feeling of anger at the fact that one's identity and group affiliation are either denied by the wider society or not given sufficient recognition in its politics. The implication for liberal-democracy then is that the whole concept of democratic public space has to be rethought, with greater recognition of the need for both separation and unity. The democratic community must allow space, both metaphorical and literal, for adherents of a particular culture to express their identity and their beliefs yet at the same time develop links with their fellow-citizens in order to prevent those feelings of isolation and resentment which fuel violence. This in turn is related to the process of globalisation, which stimulates insecurity resulting from the spread of a market-driven society throughout the world, and from which no section of society on a global level is immune. The spread of neo-liberal practices means that the nation-state, which used to function as an integrating set of institutions to bring citizens together in a civic community, is undermined or hampered in that function by the world-wide spread of a market society which erodes previous forms of solidarity.

The spread of globalisation also undermines a situation in which individuals are predominantly situated in self-contained communities joined together by a common culture and relatively insulated from other cultures. The outcome of a globalised world is a much more 'cheek by jowl' kind of society in which each member is confronted on a daily basis by the presence of other cultures and by those affiliated to other identities. The consequence of such a situation is that there are greater opportunities for 'disrespect', for confrontations between holders of different identities, each of them in a position of greater insecurity because of the weakness of the formerly integrative institutions of the nation-state. These, then, are the factors which unsettle citizens and predispose them to a readiness to violent action and to sympathy with those undertaking such action.

If terrorism as a political problem, both within particular states and on a global scale, arises out of these general causes, then what would be the shape of the 'equal and opposite' reaction to terrorism? As we have suggested, such a reaction would need to be based on democratic principles themselves rather than on treating terrorism as a security problem to be met through the violence of the state. If the analysis given here is correct, terrorism is a pathological symptom of the fact that all is not well with the liberal-democratic state, so that attention has to be switched to righting its defects. Such defects furnish the basis for terrorism in that they allow terrorists to claim that their action is necessary to rectify the 'historic grievance' perpetrated, and also perpetuated, by the liberal-democratic state. Hence the first step in a democratic and political reaction to terrorism must be to at least acknowledge the existence of the problem to which terrorist groups are pointing. Governments and citizens of the liberal-democratic society have to show their awareness of the issue which terrorism is highlighting, in order to counter the claim that violence is the only means through which such awareness and discussion of the issue can be achieved.

Clearly this is to make some rather optimistic assumptions; they are not, however, wholly unrealistic. In the first place the assumption is that terrorist actions are carried out with some definite end in view, an end which could be articulated and which would entail policy changes and institutional transformations which in principle could be accepted by the citizens of a transformed democracy. This holds out the possibility, at some stage, of dialogue and reciprocal discussion concerning the goals of those practising violence, and the possible rectification of grievances which could be achieved within the framework of a democratic society. The problem with this perspective is that it is difficult to apply to terrorist actions –such as those of Al Qaeda, exemplified by the events of 9/11 – whose demands seem, at least in part, to involve the abolition of the democratic system itself and a condemnation of its whole theoretical basis. The analysis of terrorism as an appeal for inclusion and recognition does not appear to apply here. Yet the idea noted above, of 'disaggregating' terrorism as a political movement and set of problems, has to be borne in mind here too. While some of the reasons or goals set out by terrorist organisations are not such as could be accepted by the citizens or governments of any democratic society, others are more concrete – for example, the demand that Western governments reduce their intervention, especially their military presence, in Muslim lands. While it is naïve to suggest that discussion will by some magic cure transform terrorists into democratic interlocutors, the analysis offered here suggests that a minimum condition for beginning such a process would be for the governments and citizens of a democracy to ask those practising terrorist action for the rationale behind their actions. What is terrorist action meant to achieve? It seems that one statement on which the voluminous literature on terrorism is in agreement is that those who are involved in such use of violence are not, in general, psychologically disturbed or any less rational than 'ordinary' citizens. The implication of this is that terrorism is a rational political strategy designed to achieve certain ends. Those ends must, on a minimal assumption of human rationality, be capable of being stated and articulated, at least if terrorists are to offer any justification for their actions.

It has to be repeated that this is not to offer a moral justification for acts of terrorism, but only to investigate further in what ways it challenges democratic society and how that challenge is to be met. If violence is to be steered into democratic channels, then the first prerequisite is to listen to the demands made by those engaged in terrorist action, and for governments to debate with their citizens the nature of those demands and open up for public discussion the question of the extent to which they might be addressed within the framework of a democratic society. This implies that terrorist action should be brought before a (metaphorical) 'court of public opinion', and it is in that sense that the idea of an 'equal and opposite reaction', sketched out above, is proposed. If a convincing case can be made that there could be democratic reforms which achieve, if only in part, the ends claimed by those carrying out acts of terrorism, this could lead to the diminution, or even the disappearance, of any residual sympathy for terrorist activity among wider sections of the citizen body. This would be all the more likely if the ends aimed at by terrorists could with any plausibility be claimed to be 'defects' of the particular liberal-democratic society in question and remediable by means other than those of violence.

As we have seen, in practice this would mean the practices and institutions of liberal-democratic society would have to change. The argument presented here does not imply that when faced with the use of violence by terrorist groups the liberal-democratic state should not effectively defend the security of its citizens. It does imply, however, that the problems which terrorist violence raises, or the grievances which are exploited by its 'political entrepreneurs', have to be brought to the attention of a wider public by governments, so that there can be a genuine debate about how such problems and grievances might be met. This is not to suggest that there is or could be an easy solution to such issues, or even that they might be settled within the framework of the democratic community as presently constituted. Terrorism is often concerned with problematic issues of who belongs to the democratic community, leading to claims of nationalism, secession and the recognition of distinct cultures and identities. Groups using violence claim, in certain cases, that the democratic community as presently constituted is oppressive and does not allow recognition of a national minority. Thus the use of violence is often directed to demands that would entail the break-up of the democratic community in its existing form. This applies, for example, in the case of Basque terrorism, whose demands are for an independent Basque nation-state which would take regions from both France and Spain to constitute an independent 'Euskadi'. Hence public discussion on this particular issue has to question the bases of the democratic community in France and Spain respectively, by raising the topic of recognition of distinct national cultures which coexist within those states. These states can no longer be called nation-states if that term is taken to denote a state with a single and homogenous national culture.

In the present order of liberal-democracy, forums for the wider discussion of such problems either do not exist or are limited to the formal representative institutions of the state. If terrorism is treated purely as a security problem then this tends to limit more open discussion of the issue it raises, since it is presented purely as a problem of securing the safety of citizens. This is too partial a perspective since it deflects attention from any rational end aspired to by terrorist groups, and the validity of their claim that it is only by means of fear and terror than the issue can be brought to the attention of democratic citizens. This claim can only be shown to be false, and the justification for terrorism thereby removed, if there is a wide-ranging presentation of the issue to the public. This process is made more difficult if the issue is treated in purely security terms.

If three of the central causes of terrorism can be summarised under the headings of religion, nationalism and social deprivation, then the phenomenon of terrorism can be understood as an appeal to democratic public opinion to address these issues. Terrorists make the claim that the structure of liberal-democracy in its present form denies the possibility of any solution to, and indeed the opportunity for, extended discussion of the issues most at stake for them. Terrorism is thus always an inherent possibility within democratic politics. It is a challenge in the sense that it demands that democratic societies live up to their principles of ensuring free and equal recognition and some degree of economic and social equality. To say this is not to justify terrorism, still less to glorify it, but to seek to explain why it happens and how democratic societies should respond to it, consistent with their own foundational principles. The idea of restoring democratic community is better understood as a challenge to restructure it. Were such a restructuring to be undertaken successfully, violence would be unnecessary and resorted to by only a few pathological individuals, since the aims sought by means of violence could be pursued within the framework of the democratic order. No convincing case could then be made for the necessity of violence.

To work towards this desirable situation the framework of liberal-democracy has to be transformed through the development of institutions which permit and encourage the greater involvement of minority groups. This could restore some of the power of the nation-state to guarantee the solidarity previously enjoyed by its members, currently weakened through the spread of globalisation and its emphasis on the market. Terrorism has sparked off a reaction in which the state increases the power of its security organs, thereby only perpetuating or continuing the cycle of violence rather than ending it. The correct strategy for ending violence or marginalising it as a political weapon is to pay attention to the grievances used to justify it, and to make plausible the claim that these grievances can be and are being addressed through democratic means, thus undermining the terrorist claim that violence is needed to place them on the agenda of public opinion.

5 Ethnic and Nationalist Violence and Democracy

This chapter seeks to explain in what ways nationalism, understood broadly as the sense of belonging to a community having its own history, culture and territory (or claiming such), is a fundamental cause of violence in contemporary politics, and in what ways nationalist violence might be 'contained' (Hechter 2000) or even removed as a cause of political violence in the world.

This has to be related to the guiding themes of the present book, whose core ideas are that violence arises out of two main factors, the first being exclusion or lack of recognition, the second nationalist oppression or lack of 'fit' between nation and state. This can be explained further as meaning that the state lacks legitimacy in the eyes of members of a particular nation, because the state does not recognise the culture of that nation, and refuses to concede it any autonomy or self-government. This chapter seeks to explain under what conditions nationalist grievances turn to violence. The obvious examples include those of Basque nationalism and the conflict in Ireland between republican nationalists and the majority (in Northern Ireland) wanting to retain their membership of the United Kingdom. There are other examples, such as the wave of nationalist mobilisation which accompanied the collapse of the Soviet Union. Within that sub-category one can place the case of Chechnya, itself cause of a bloody war with the Soviet Union and then with Russia, or secessionist and separatist movements like those in East Timor demanding independence from Indonesia.

It is clear that nationalism does not necessarily lead to violence, since one could list as counter-examples many cases where nationalist demands have been made without violence resulting, such as the case of Scotland, or Catalonia. In these cases some *modus vivendi* has been worked out, so that cultural and political autonomy allows for the satisfaction of nationalist demands within the framework of a larger national, or rather multi-national, unit. Nevertheless, what is to be analysed is how contemporary liberal-democratic societies need to respond to nationalist and ethnic issues to prevent such demands from promoting violent conflict, as they have done in several cases, including those mentioned above. Two possible solutions can be sketched out. The first can be labelled *cosmopolitan*, in which nationalism is transcended or superseded by other more extensive loyalties. The second is a solution which uses nationalism to drive out nationalism. In this case a more comprehensive civic type of nationalism, which could be described as a lighter or toned-down nationalism, acts to focus civic loyalty and restrain the tendency of stronger forms of nationalism to take violent paths.

Why Does Nationalism Lead to Violence?

Two hypotheses explain the tendency of nationalist ideas and movements to lead to violence. The first arises out of globalisation and the resulting insecurity it creates for certain sections of the population. According to Gellner, one of the characteristics of nationalism is the simplicity of its ideas (Gellner 1983: 124): as an ideology, nationalism lacks any heavyweight thinkers or philosophers. This judgement can be contested, since there are thinkers who have sought to develop a philosophy of nationalism. However, nationalism, in the simplistic sense of an attachment to a national community perceived as having its own history, culture and identity, can function as a sort of politics of the lowest common denominator. A feeling of national identity functions as a bonding device linking people together. Such a sentiment of national togetherness is often heightened by identifying an out-group, an 'Other' against whom the 'in-group' can be defined.

This is indeed no sophisticated philosophy, but in such cases nationalism can serve as a sort of lightning-conductor for insecurities stemming from economic or more general social causes. In conditions of a globalised world, the former homogeneity of the nation-state no longer exists, or at least does so in far weaker form. Those who previously found security in identifying with what could be claimed to be their traditions and culture – which provided them with a solidity and a base of recognisable features (the traditions of their nation) – can no longer do so, since those traditions are now challenged by minority groups and other cultures, brought together by the pressures of globalisation.

Nationalist violence is stimulated in these cases by two factors, in a kind of 'push and pull' relationship. A globalised world leads to greater insecurity, especially for those whose skills are no longer in demand in the post-industrial economy. Globalisation is good for some, but bad for others. Those in the latter category are less able than they once were to seek effective compensation for that insecurity in the protective embrace of a solid national culture and identity with its familiar symbols and rituals. Such familiar reference points have been eroded by a global culture as well as by hybrid mixtures of different cultures and societies. This can stimulate forms of xenophobic nationalism which seek to vent hostility on certain scapegoats or targets who are blamed in an incoherent way for the economic and social insecurity arising out of globalisation. Such insecurity can be exploited and mobilised by right-wing movements using nationalism of this kind to ground the sense of dissatisfaction and fear felt by groups dislocated or threatened by global developments. Violence arises when threatened groups have their insecurities manipulated by such movements, using these themes of national culture being threatened by outsiders and immigrants of various kinds. Hence nationalist violence emerges in xenophobic form, manifesting itself in aggression towards an 'Other', and in extremist attempts to safeguard what is often a mythical form of 'true' national identity seen as undermined by an influx of foreign elements and adherents of different cultures.

There is nothing new about such developments, since these forms of potentially violent xenophobic nationalism can be identified at least as far back as the late nineteenth century. France provides some good examples of hostility to the *déracinés* and immigrants who were portrayed as responsible for national decline and disintegration. A populist nationalism, with its constant incitement to violence against these scapegoats, was exemplified by movements like *le parti nationaliste* of the Third French Republic (Girardet 1966). This was not really a party in the strict sense but more a set of movements, vehemently anti-parliamentary and demagogic in tone, calling for a new and more authoritarian political order to replace what was seen as the ineffective parliamentary system. In the period of the Third French Republic theorists and political leaders like Maurice Barrès and Charles Maurras exploited the theme of the Jew and the foreign worker polluting the essence of the French nation.

Nevertheless, even if there is nothing inherently new about such developments, it can be said that they have been intensified by globalisation and its consequences, which deepen the insecurity for which this kind of populist and xenophobic nationalism is seen as a solution. Such insecurity leads to violent aggression if it is channelled in that direction by parties and movements which direct attention to scapegoats or identify an 'Other' as the cause of the felt grievances. If the nation-state no longer functions as an adequate 'protector' of its members, then the (ethnically defined) 'core' citizens may seek to go back to a largely mythical vision of a culturally cohesive nation-state with reassuring criteria of national identity. However, since in reality this is no longer available, the search for a security that is not forthcoming gives rise to fear, even to violence when the absence of the reassuring nation-state can be blamed on an identifiable target, the figure of the foreigner, the immigrant, now portrayed as destroying the cohesion of the nation. The accelerated scope of movement and the greater heterogeneity of cultures within the territory of particular nations make this problem more acute in the contemporary world. Hence violence becomes more likely as the expression of such xenophobic nationalism, as outbursts of opposition to groups defined as different in culture, religion, and identity. They are blamed for the problems which are in truth the result of the destructive forces of globalisation and the extension of the market to areas of life previously protected from market forces.

Social-democratic parties were able in an earlier period to socialise the nation to a certain degree, in line with the statement of the historian E. H. Carr that 'the nationalisation of socialism has as its corollary the socialisation of the nation' (Carr 1968: 19). By 'socialisation of the nation' is to be understood the penetration of the nation by social-democratic forces using the national framework to install a welfare state and integrate the working-class into the nation. Such a perspective was held out by the Austro-Marxist theorist Otto Bauer in his great study *The Question of Nationalities and Social Democracy* in which he wrote that socialism would mean that the mass of the population, hitherto excluded from the national culture, could become drawn into full membership of the nation (Bauer 2000 [1924]). This membership would be cultural but also economic, guaranteed by a welfare state which ironed out the inequalities of the market through social policy and an ability and willingness to steer the economy in bad times.

While such perspectives have not totally disappeared, they are considerably weakened in the contemporary epoch of globalisation and the flow of economic power away from the nation-state. The socialisation of the nation is no longer such a powerful or attractive programme because the nation-state is less effective as a container or vessel of economic power. Thus Habermas is right to suggest that in what he calls 'the postnational constellation' a new closure or *Schliessung* is needed, to establish control over a new globalised area of economic power (Habermas 2001). Whereas in the national constellation the nation-state, resting on a relatively homogeneous national culture (*Volksnation*), was able to 'discipline' or to some extent control the forces of economic life, this is less so in the so-called postnational constellation. Therefore, a new supra-national set of institutions (according to Habermas) would be needed to achieve the closure formerly secured by the nation-state. Such a *Schliessung* would involve the creation of institutions of cosmopolitan democracy (Archibugi 2008).

However, in the world as it is such a supra-national closure has not yet been achieved and the security, both economic and cultural, previously provided by the nation-state is a thing of the past. The comforting symbols of national identity no longer function to bring citizens together in a community both psychologically satisfying and also genuinely effective in providing a degree of social security and mutual recognition. A number of consequences flow from this. The desire still exists for national security, not in the sense in which that phrase is used in international relations, but as denoting a situation where a certain degree of protection is provided by the nation-state. Since the desire exists but is not satisfied, the resulting dissatisfaction finds expression in a form of nationalism making some identifiable group responsible for the multicultural and diverse character of the nation from which the familiar safety-nets have disappeared. The eruption of violent nationalism, or the turning of nationalism into violent xenophobic forms, is explained in this way. It is a result of anger (Sloterdijk 2006) over the fact that the national community is no longer present in the same forms as earlier, to provide psychological and social security. This anger, especially if it is mobilised and heightened by political leaders and parties of the radical right, then turns against some identifiable scapegoat, the blaming of whom is easier to understand than the problems of international finance and globalised markets.

In such ways nationalism feeds violence directed against those of other cultures and identities living 'cheek by jowl' on the same national territory. The two solutions identified above need to be examined as possible routes out of the tendency of nationalism to be violent: *either* a cosmopolitan '*Schliessung*' or closure appropriate to the postnational constellation, *or* the development (or redevelopment) of the national idea in civic or republican forms to make nationalism a factor which fosters community rather than conflict. The problem with nationalism is that it fosters conflict at the same time as it provides a sense of community. Indeed, the community which it engenders in at least some of its forms is itself a factor in generating conflict, since the sense of unity is often enhanced by opposition to an outside group. In that way, since community is purchased through conflict, it is difficult to see how a strong sense of national identity can be made compatible with the conflicts and diversity that characterise contemporary societies.

Nationalist Oppression and Violence

What was said above relates to a nationalism of insecurity within the context of established liberal-democratic societies. There is another category of cases where nationalism turns to violence in a global context. The cases relevant here are those of nationalist oppression, which involves the lack of recognition of a particular national culture and its consequent exclusion from full civic or citizenship rights. Where a particular ethnic or national group is a minority part of a state which gives more rights to the majority culture, such a situation combines oppression with exclusion and lack of recognition. The particular characteristic of nationalist conflict which raises problems for democratic theory and practice stems from the cultural dimension which is essential to nationalism. The analysis of democracy and violence given here assumes that violence can be 'steered' into channels of democratic debate and reconciliation, with compromise achieved through discussion between citizens who recognise each other as equally entitled to participate in democratic dialogue. It is clear that this is an idealised and theoretical description of democracy, but it describes the aspiration of a society of equals who deliberate in common.

This deliberately idealised picture of democracy relies on the assumption that there is a consensus on procedures. This involves agreement on the processes of deliberation and the ways in which a decision is arrived at. Such a consensus should command the assent, however reluctant, of the citizens of a democratic order.

Yet it rests on one further assumption which is equally important: an assumption concerning who the citizens of the polity are. In this sense Nodia is right to say that nationalism is but another name for 'we the people' (Nodia 1994). It offers an answer to the question of what group of people constitutes the 'team' which plays by the democratic rules of the game: who are the citizens? Yet again, nationalism is a possible solution or answer as well as a potential problem in this regard. Nationalism offers an answer to the question of 'who are the citizens?' of the polity in question, by responding that it is the members of the nation who form the citizen body. Yet this is clearly problematic in cases where there is more than one national group within the state or polity. If the state comprises more than one nation and if the state is defined as being the state of one (majority) national group, then members of the other national group or groups subject to the same state are denied recognition and the status of full members of the citizen body. This is evidently a situation which can lead to violence and that presents particular problems for the view of democracy given here. This view suggested that in a full democracy issues could be debated between citizens who respect each other and grant each other the status of citizens. It suggests furthermore that there is a possibility of compromise and of the reconciliation of differences.

However, it is the distinctive characteristic of nationalist conflict to make both these aspects of a democratic society highly problematic. If members of one national group refuse to grant the members of another such group the status of citizens, or at least refuse to accept them as citizens on equal terms, then democratic deliberation between equals is evidently impossible. Furthermore, if the issues are those of cultural recognition and the acceptance of difference, then these are questions on which it is difficult to reach a compromise, since they are often of an all-or-nothing character. Either the particular national group is given the right to practise its culture, or it is denied such a right. This perhaps is too stark a picture: there is no doubt room for debate between different cultures and identities, and it is true that no particular identity or culture is totally uniform. To take one example, if one cultural or national group has practices which deny women equal rights in a legal sense with men, this group would not, in a liberal-democratic society, be allowed to continue with such practices. Yet it could continue with other practices which do not go against the fundamental beliefs of a liberal-democratic society. Nevertheless, strong cultural and national differences present a challenge for democratic society since they raise issues of identity and belief on which compromise decisions are harder to envisage. Minority national groups accused by the majority of being 'disloyal' to the state of which they are part will in fact turn out to be so if they are denied the right to their language and other cultural practices. If they see no chance of achieving autonomy or some degree of self-rule, then violence may be the only way in which their grievances can be expressed, since they may be or feel themselves to be in a permanent minority. Thus there would be no chance of this minority national group achieving the satisfaction of its aims through democratic channels and institutions allowing peaceful debate and reconciliation of contentious issues, because the minority group is not recognised as being of equal citizen status and hence cannot participate in any such debate.

The violence exercised by nationalist groups may be aimed at a variety of goals, including secession, autonomy or devolution. Secession obviously involves separation from the state unit of which the national group is part. This is more likely to involve violence because of the loss of territory, resources and prestige to the state from which the nationalist movement wishes to secede. In that situation the case for secession has to be a strong one, given the resistance which it is likely to provoke from the larger state. In addition, there is one further danger with secessionist movements, namely that, if the secessionist movement is successful, the newly formed unit will find within its new state another minority who, if they are oppressed, will in their turn embark on a fight for secession, perhaps by violent means too. There is thus a permanent dynamic within nationalist and cultural demands that tends towards violence. One group seeks recognition and freedom from the oppression of another national group, yet having secured its own freedom it can in its turn develop into an equally oppressive force towards a minority in the newly seceded state. The former domination of Serbs over Kosovan Albanians in what used to be Kosovo as part of Serbia has turned into a situation where the Serbs, now in a minority in the quasi-independent state of Kosovo, are themselves a victimised group.

Nationalism is thus 'twinned' with violence in two kinds of cases. The first is that of a defensive or reactive nationalism, a nationalism of fear where insecurities arising out of globalisation find expression in a xenophobic populist nationalism directed against a scapegoat or targeted minority group. The other form is that of a national or ethnic group which is oppressed and feels its culture and identity are not recognised by the state of which it is part. This is not to say that violent conflict is inevitable, but unless there is some recognition of the problem, by which is meant a degree of political or cultural autonomy, violent secession remains likely. Of course, this depends on a range of factors affecting the 'secession potential' in the particular case. The term 'secession potential' is used by Hughes in his study of the Chechnya case (Hughes 2007). He lists five factors as crucial in affecting the likelihood of secession. The first is the demographic composition of the potentially seceding unit – 'the presence of a territorially concentrated and dissatisfied minority group'. If there is such a group present, as there was in Chechnya which had 'one of the largest absolute majorities of any titular ethnic group in its own territory' (Hughes 2007: 33), this makes secession more likely. To this factor must be added the question of whether the potentially seceding unit has important economic resources of its own and whether it is geographically remote from the centre of the state from which it might secede, or whether its location is 'close to the core of the federal state' (Hughes 2007: 36). Finally there is the factor of the degree of identity and assimilation. Does the potentially seceding unit have a tradition of independent statehood and historical legacies, however myth-like, on which it could rely as the basis for a renewed attempt at independence, using the past record of statehood as a legitimating ideology in this regard? The attitude of the state from which secession is contemplated is also of significance: if the central state sees the potentially seceding unit as inherently part of its territory and bound to it, then secessionist moves will be met with much greater resistance. This was the case in Chechnya where 'the Chechens . . . have been forced into a violent struggle to secede from Russia, and consequently have mobilised more around ethno-religious myths of the nineteenth century and Islamist resistance to Russian imperial conquest' (Hughes 2007: 37).

Two Possible Solutions

If nationalism fosters political violence in such ways, the question is how such nationalist conflict could be made compatible with the processes and institutions of democracy. The two broad forms outlined above (defensive nationalism and secessionist nationalism) arise in two distinct contexts: the first is that of established liberal-democracy where social strata are made insecure as a result of globalisation and its economic impact. The second is one where nationalist cleavages, whether in an established or a would-be democracy, undermine the sense of community needed for a functioning democratic society. How strong such a community has to be is the subject of much debate. If nationalist cleavages make impossible the mutual recognition of citizens as equally entitled to participate in democratic dialogue, then the processes of democracy cannot be realised in practice. The problem is then how to achieve this degree of mutual recognition and community needed for a functioning democratic society. If community and conflict are inherent features of a democratic society, then nationalist conflict is especially problematic in this regard because it involves issues of identity and culture on which compromise is difficult. Compromise is difficult because if the state is the state of one particular nation with a distinct cultural and national identity to which it gives priority, then recognition of sub-cultures or of minority identities may be seen as threatening the integrity or the unity of the whole state. As Kymlicka points out, the idea of a culturally or ethnically neutral state is impossible to achieve (Kymlicka 2001: 24). Since most states today are in fact ethnically and nationally diverse, how then can democracy function in such multi-national democracies?

Here again the problem arises out of the changed conditions of world politics, since the classical idea of the nation-state with one culture and one identity, presided over by a single state, has long ceased to be a reality in contemporary conditions. It is true that it never was a complete reality, so that nationalism of the classical kind, defined by Gellner as the idea of the cultural unit of the nation coinciding with the political unit of the state, has always been a myth (Gellner 1998). The idea of a single unified culture has never been realised in practice to any complete degree. Yet diversity and the hybrid nature of different cultures are both salient features of contemporary politics which find expression in the eruption of national and cultural conflicts. One response to these problems is the cosmopolitan one. A cosmopolitan solution involves the idea of a democracy in which national and cultural markers or distinctions are irrelevant and in which states seek to be culturally neutral, protecting the rights of citizens irrespective of their national or cultural affiliation. This does not entail the idea of world government or the dissolution of nation-states, but refers to a conception of multi-national democratic societies which combines two features. On the one hand it involves the recognition of distinct cultures and identities as basic factors in giving people their sense of who they are. On the other hand it requires an ideal of citizen identity which is not dependent on any particular cultural identity or set of beliefs. Each individual is a citizen irrespective of their grounding in or adherence to a particular culture or group.

This is a different interpretation of cosmopolitanism from others in the literature, since cosmopolitanism is conventionally taken to mean an indifference to any cultural belonging. It often refers to the wish to rise above particular identities which are experienced as limiting and constraining, in other words to be a man or woman of the world in the words of the old Latin tag '*ubi bene, ibi patria*' – wherever one feels at home, there is one's fatherland. Yet the idea of cosmopolitanism is used here in a different sense to suggest a world of states in which distinct cultures are recognised and their adherents are allowed on equal terms space to exercise their beliefs and express their particular culture. However, the sphere of the political is one which rises above that cultural sphere so that the state aspires to secure in an impartial way individuals' rights and to develop a culture of common citizenship. The crucial point is that nationalist violence can be overcome with policies of cultural autonomy in the framework of a concept of shared citizenship, with suitable institutions in place to realise this idea of shared citizenship in practice. Cosmopolitanism in this sense needs to be redefined in contrast to its more commonly accepted meaning of indifference to or even contempt for particular cultures. It implies in this redefined sense an acceptance of the plurality and necessity of distinct cultures combined with the attempt to prevent any one of them from being favoured by the state and imposed by state policy, since such partiality is a likely cause of violent nationalist conflict.

The second solution to the problem is one in which nationalism drives out nationalism, though what is involved here may not be so different in practice from what was called above the cosmopolitan solution. If nationalist conflict stems from lack of recognition of distinct identities, this second solution seeks to build up the community which reconciles the different conflicts through a form of non-ethnic nationalism based on the idea of shared citizenship values. This then reverts to the familiar distinction between civic and ethnic nationalism, but is different from the cosmopolitanism analysed above in that it emphasises a form of democratic community marked by a shared history and common civic values, seen as related to the particular traditions of the nation in question. The recent attempt in British politics to develop a British equivalent of 4th July in the USA or the 14th July in France as a symbol of multi-national solidarity would be one practical expression of this kind of policy. This differs from the approach of cosmopolitanism only in that more explicit attempts are made to elevate a concept of democratic citizenship and anchor it in the particular traditions of a historically based national community. The difference between the two positions of cosmopolitanism and nationalism driving out nationalism is well captured by Patchen Markell in his critique of Habermas' idea of constitutional patriotism, understood as the allegiance to common rights and a sense of shared allegiance to a constitution as the basis of the civic order. Markell suggests that this idea may be too thin (Markell 2000). An idea of civic community should be more firmly located in the particular traditions of a nation so that its citizens can make those universal values their own by linking them to a more limited territory and a particular history. A form of civic nationalism could prevent nationalist violence from breaking out because it would, if successful, attract the allegiance of citizens, whatever their particular cultural affinities, to a common narrative of shared rights asserted over a long period of time in opposition to foreign rule.

The question is therefore how successful such a rallying form of nationalism might be in overcoming the violent tendencies of nationalist conflict. It is clear that the success of such a narrative of civic nationalism could only be achieved if accompanied by institutional reform, by political structures which give autonomy and freedom of expression to those sharing a particular cultural identity. Therefore, the solution of civic nationalism would entail a reform in the discourse of politics which would only make sense if accompanied by institutional transformations in the structure of the polity, appropriate to the conditions of a multi-national democracy. The violence which nationalist issues engender can in fact be steered into the paths of peaceful reconciliation through this double strategy of changed discourse and institutional reform.

Problems of the Two Solutions

Nationalism thus leads to violence where people's insecurities on the one hand, and the lack of recognition of a distinct culture or national identity on the other, both undermine the citizen solidarity and mutual recognition necessary for democracy to function. The solution lies in divorcing citizen rights from their association with a particular national culture (what was called above a 'cosmopolitan' solution) while at the same time giving recognition to the practices of particular cultural or national groups. The purpose of the present section is to deepen these arguments by seeking to explain what they might mean in practice, and to suggest how it might be possible to break the 'circle of violence' (Benjamin) often associated with nationalist demands. The problem is a particularly acute one both for existing democracies and for those societies in which democracy is something still to be achieved. In the former, the greater salience of different identities and cultural group affiliations makes it more difficult to achieve the mutual recognition seen here as constitutive of democratic citizenship. If citizens are divided by distinct identities and if those identities or the groups which articulate and represent them come high in the list of attachments which individuals form, then it becomes a harder task to create a wider sense of citizen solidarity which transcends those particular loyalties. Furthermore, the particular loyalties which individuals form may turn to violence under certain conditions. If individuals feel those particular affiliations are not given sufficient respect and adequate 'space' (literally and metaphorically) to express themselves, this provides fertile ground for hostility and violence to arise between different cultural and ethnic groups in a given society. Riots in British cities (like Bradford) exemplify this potential for conflicting identities to generate violent confrontation, and those who feel threatened seek an illusory satisfaction in violent antagonism towards some 'out-group' which can be blamed for the lack of respect or low status felt by the supposedly aggrieved group.

This is not meant to suggest that established democracies with their multicultural citizen composition are in imminent danger of exploding into violent confrontation. However, it does highlight the difficulties involved in establishing the preconditions for a healthy democracy. The problem of nationalism is that in many of its forms it elevates cultural identity into a very significant 'marker' of individual value and belonging, and thus in a society made up of such different 'markers' it becomes more difficult to establish the kind of overriding citizen identity which forms the basis for an effective democracy.

With those societies where the possibility of establishing democracy is on the agenda, the problem is equally hard to overcome. In cases such as Kosovo, East Timor and present-day Iraq, violence is the 'twin' of nationalism because the state is seen as the vehicle for imposing the values of one particular national or cultural group, and therefore minority national groups have been victimised in the sense of not being given full citizenship status. To move from such a situation to one in which the state becomes the forum in which citizens debate on equal terms irrespective of their national or cultural affiliation requires a break with the past traditions of the state and with the very basis of state loyalty, rooted in the idea of defending the identity of a particular national or cultural group. That idea has itself been deeply rooted in the whole tradition of the modern state. The result is that where the homogeneity of a cultural group is no longer a valid or inclusive basis for state power and legitimacy, nationalist groups react in potentially violent ways. Those who have hitherto regarded the state as the state of 'their' group may act in aggressive ways to try and preserve this situation, even though it is no longer practicable to do so. Those groups in the minority may also act violently, perhaps pursuing secessionist forms of political action, because they see no way in which they could be recognised as citizens by a state so imbued with the cultural values of a majority culture or nationality. As in the case of Chechnya, if the state in which the minority has hitherto lived (the Russian state, in this case) sees the minority region as essential to its territory and interests, then the chances of recognition for the minority nation are correspondingly reduced.

Nationalism thus highlights the theme of the problematic character of community and conflict. Nationalism has been associated with violence and continues to be so, because it shows in a particularly clear way the demand for recognition of a cultural identity and the likelihood of violence if such recognition is not forthcoming. Nationalism is also prone to fuel violence for other reasons too, well-noted in the existing literature. The simplicity of nationalist argument or cultural affiliation ('us' versus 'them'), allied to the use of symbols and the affective or emotional aspects of nationalism, make it prone to unleash violent political action. This is especially true of situations where those sharing a particular identity feel they are not recognised by the state of which they are part, or in more extreme mode when nationalist oppression fuels resentment and the desire for a state to act as the defender of the cultural and national group in question. Since Palestinians feel that the Israeli state does not recognise their distinct identity, they resort to violence and seek to establish a state of their own, which then fuels the cycle of violence in Israel/Palestine. If two national groups demand the same territory as land for their state, with the state seen as the instrument for defending their cultural identity, then violence is the inevitable outcome.

Historically, the nation-state acted as a defensive buffer protecting the national culture from the outside world. In the view of some nationalists, like Johann Fichte, it was the task of the state to preserve the nation from 'contamination' by a foreign culture (Fichte 1979). Fichte saw such an alien culture exemplified by France, which in his view had tried to 'infect' German identity with such words as 'humanity' and 'liberality' which could not legitimately find any home in the German language. Not all those who insist on the link between the state and a particular national culture do so in the closed and extreme forms which Fichte defended, with his idea of an original or '*Ur-kultur*' whose distinctive character has to be preserved in an integral form. This idea resurfaced later, ironically in France, the very country seen by Fichte as the would-be bearer of universal values. 'Integral' nationalists like Maurras and Barrès maintained a view not so different from that held by Fichte a century earlier across the Rhine. They saw the task of the state as one of defending a 'pure' national culture from foreign infection, a culture threatened by the four estates (as Maurras termed them) of the immigrant (*métèque*), the Jew, the freemasons and the Protestants. Individuals belonging to such groups could not be true members of the 'real' French nation, even though they might somehow have attained the status of legal membership (*le pays réel* versus *le pays légal*).

Understood in such integral or extreme terms this identification of the state with the nation often leads to violence, since it purchases community (very tightly defined as a community of birth or descent which no 'foreigner' can join) at the expense of the outsider or alien. This is therefore incompatible with any notion of democracy or democratic community. In contemporary conditions the association of the state with a particular culture raises a similar danger of nationalism fostering violence, since it leads to the two related problems of exclusion from the democratic community and nationalist oppression. While it is historically accurate to portray the modern nation-state as existing on the basis of a distinct national culture and having the task of protecting that culture, there is no reason to see this as continuing in the situation of contemporary politics, given the fact that such a common national culture is no longer a feature of contemporary societies. This is itself a result of globalisation and of population flows, which bring together in close proximity people with diverse cultural affiliations. This argument echoes Habermas' perspective that the cultural 'substratum' of what he calls the *Volksnation* is no longer available in the contemporary world, whose political unity has to be achieved through the *Bürgernation* or civil nation (Habermas 2001).

The modern state has thus to satisfy two conflicting needs, if there is to be any chance of minimising the recourse to violence which stems from exclusion or national oppression. The first need is for the recognition of distinct cultures and national identities, since failure to respect distinct cultures leads to violence. It signifies that the state and political society generally are not disposed to accept as citizens on equal terms those who are attached to a particular minority culture. The second need, equally important from the point of view of avoiding violence, is for some overarching civic identity which not only prevents violent conflict between members of different cultural groups, but which fosters those ideas of democratic community that are essential for a democracy to work. The association of the political state with the cultural (national) community runs the risk of excluding those who do not share the dominant ethnic or cultural identity which historically has underpinned the state. Hence the state stimulates violence rather than fulfilling the role of steering conflict away from violent confrontation into peaceful channels of compromise and reconciliation. This task becomes more difficult as long as the state is associated with a dominant culture, because it is then perceived as hostile or not receptive to the bearers of different cultures.

There has to be some attempt to 'denationalise' the state, to create state institutions which at one and the same time concede recognition of culture and identity to particular groups while simultaneously not giving privileges to any one cultural or national affiliation. This goes against the line of argument which maintains the impossibility of a culturally neutral state, given the historical links between the state and a particular national culture which formed the basis of the state and secured citizens' loyalty to it. As already noted, this may well have been the case historically, but is no longer the imperative of present-day politics, particularly since associating state and (dominant) cultural group in this way only exacerbates the risks of violence. The solution proposed here is for a kind of parallel to the secularisation of the state and its separation of politics from religion. This put an end to the religious wars of the seventeenth century by making religion a private matter. In the case of nationalism and violence, the present argument takes inspiration from the Austro-Marxist ideas of 'cultural autonomy', presented at the beginning of the twentieth century in the very different circumstances of the Austro-Hungarian Empire. In that context different national groups struggled for both cultural and political recognition, with the result that nationalist struggles paralysed the political life of the Empire which the socialists wished to preserve. One of the leading Austro-Marxists, Karl Renner, in his pamphlet *State and Nation* advocated the separation of 'nation' from 'state' (Renner 2005). According to him, the nation was a cultural association and therefore appropriate cultural institutions should be created so that each national group would run its own cultural affairs, partly through the control of local government. In contrast, the state would be the sphere where questions of both political rights and economic and social policy would be debated and decided, irrespective of ethnic or cultural affiliation. For Renner, as a Marxist, it would be social classes which would be the main players in the field of state policy. The benefits of cultural autonomy would be that national pride and recognition of identity would be secured through the pluralist self-organisation of the different national communities. Political life could progress without being envenomed by the demands of national groups for recognition and cultural rights. In this way, it was hoped, national demands would be satisfied and 'contained' (Hechter 2000) in the sphere of culture, separate from that of politics.

Of course we are not living in the time of the Austro-Hungarian monarchy, and one has to recognise that even then the policy of cultural autonomy did not succeed in taming the force of nationalist passion. The reasons for this failure lay predominantly in the fact that national groups were not satisfied with cultural autonomy but wanted a greater degree of state power (a state that was 'their' state) in order to guarantee the flourishing of their own culture and the institutions (especially educational ones) necessary to promote that culture. However, the circumstances of present-day politics are arguably more favourable to a variant of this idea of cultural autonomy. In order to prevent nationalism and cultural identity from leading to violence, there has to be recognition of different cultural identities at the same time as their transcendence in the mutual recognition of citizens irrespective of ethnic and cultural identity. This is why the requirements for such a solution to the problem are in tension with each other: there has to be both an acceptance of the diversity of citizen identities, and the assertion of a common civic loyalty in a political unit shared with others of different cultures and beliefs. But acceptance of plurality implies the abandonment of a strict requirement that all citizens share a common national culture, given the impossibility of such a culture in the circumstances of modern politics. In that respect the nationalist programme, in its classical form, is no longer relevant to the circumstances of a fundamentally transformed world. Nationalism in its classical form used to ensure solidarity between citizens based on a common culture. In that respect it did succeed in reducing violence, at least between the citizens of a common nation-state who shared the same cultural values. This was presided over by a state which fostered and reinforced such cultural solidarity through the educational system and other institutions, such as national military service and the symbolic attachment to the nation enforced through means of political socialisation. However, the solidarity forged through the nation-state and the resultant reduction of violence inside it were both often obtained by channelling this solidarity against the non-national, those who were not members of the nation, with the result that the record of the nation-state with respect to violence is two-sided. Its reduction of violence internally went along with an external increase of violence against other nations and colonised peoples, as well as against would-be members of the nation who were not seen as true members according to some versions of nationalist rhetoric.

The way out of the 'circle' of nationalist violence, therefore, is to break or weaken the historically hallowed connection between state and nation, so that nationalist violence is not fostered by state power as the instrument of one national group. Given that the 'marriage' of state and nation is no longer an appropriate match, the two (former) partners have to be placed in a new configuration. The state has to be the agency which strives to achieve solidarity and political community between the members of the polity irrespective of ethnic or cultural affiliation. The nation has to provide in a general sense the associations which cater for cultural identity, with one important proviso which distinguishes the present analysis from that offered by the Austro-Marxists. They seemed to think of national culture in rather fixed terms, so that the image they presented was of individuals being stuck in one culture represented by a range of associations and institutions catering for those who identified themselves as members of that particular culture. This is to view culture in rather a congealed way as a solid entity whose members are members of that one culture and of no other. Such a view is false if it suggests that distinct cultures exist as hermetically sealed units having no contact with one another, and if it also suggests that individuals are members or affiliates of a single culture (Benhabib 2002). Neither assumption is valid in the circumstances of contemporary politics, where different cultures and identities affect and influence each other, and where individuals derive their identity from a range of sources and cultures. The conclusion must therefore be that national and cultural groups must have a certain space and a certain guarantee of their functioning and autonomy provided by the state, subject to a degree of 'scrutiny' to ensure that minimum standards are observed. These would involve at least the following: gender equality, protection of minors, and rights of free entry to and exit from the group in question.

The aim of this chapter has thus been to show the ways in which nationalism has, both historically and in contemporary politics, fuelled and caused violence, and the difficulties which nationalism presents as a potential obstacle to democratic community. Nationalism as a political force operates with basic ideas of culture and identity, issues on which it is difficult to envisage compromise and reconciliation, especially if members of a particular group are overwhelmed with fear that their culture will not be recognised in the state of which they are members. This then leads to the mutually reinforcing dangers of secession by the minority and repression by the majority; dangers that apply both to established democracies and to democracies in the making.

Nevertheless, the link between nationalism and violence can be broken through constitutional and institutional arrangements which loosen the historically formed link between state and nation. Such a disassociation would free minority groups from the suspicion that the state is not 'their' state but an agency for enforcing an alien identity on them, or at least for refusing recognition to the multifarious cultures and identities which are an inevitable feature of the contemporary world. In this sense then, the move has to be towards multi-national democracies which challenge the form of the nation-state. The assertion here is not that the nation-state in its classical form necessarily leads to violence, but rather that in multicultural conditions where the notion of a shared common culture no longer functions, a common cultural unity is not possible. Attempts to enforce such a unity lead to violence, and that is the danger which must be averted. The institutional and political means for doing so will be developed further in the final chapter. The next chapter turns to attempts to export and impose democracy in an international setting.

6 Violence and the Installation of Democracy

This chapter seeks to broaden the analysis by switching attention to the international dimension of the problem of democracy and violence. This can be summarised with reference to two themes, both connected with globalisation and the prevalence of violence in a global setting. The use of violence for political ends is practised both by state actors and non-state actors. In a global context, the phenomenon of violence has been linked with attempts to spread democracy as a global value, to install democratic regimes world-wide through military means. Equally, violence and terror are practised by global movements which oppose the values and institutions of democracy and seek to threaten citizens of democratic societies both in their homelands and outside them. Thus violence has to be understood in this global setting.

One of the main features of the contemporary situation is how some leaders of liberal-democratic societies have seen it as their mission to bring democracy to the wider world and to do so if necessary by means of violent 'regime change'. This can be dismissed as a mask for economic interests (for example, the search for secure sources of oil, as has been alleged with reference to Iraq) or as an attempt to divert attention away from domestic problems towards international ones. Nevertheless, any study of the challenge of violence has to grapple with the problem that much of the violence in the contemporary world is carried out in the name of democracy itself. It is justified in idealistic terms as making the world 'a better place' by spreading the values and institutions of democratic politics to those areas of the world that do not enjoy such benefits. But it is also presented in more self-interested terms as contributing to the security of the established democracies by eradicating or containing the threat from non-democratic regimes and the movements protected by those regimes. Evidently, the cases of Afghanistan and Iraq are the major examples here.

If democracy can be understood as a system which aims to settle disputes and conflicts through practices of debate and reconciliation, does this justify the attempt to use violence instrumentally to create democratic systems where they do not already exist? In what ways, if any, is violent state action justified in order to bring democracy into being? Political violence in the contemporary world is associated with the actions of states justifying violent action (war) in the name of democracy as a legitimate response to movements of terror opposing democracy. The question to be answered is whether violence is necessary to create democracy in opposition to established or crumbling authoritarian rule. What can democratic political theory teach us about the use of violence justified as a necessary means for the installation or construction of a democratic system? This is not a question which can be answered in purely normative terms, because it raises issues of a more empirical kind about the possibility and the limits of 'democracy building'. If democracy involves mutual trust between citizens regarding each other as equals, then how can this trust be created in situations where it has been absent either because of a legacy of authoritarian rule or because of deep ethnic, regional or other divisions which have impeded the construction of a democratic community?

If democratic politics aims at rendering violence unnecessary since all voices would be heard in a democratic system, can violence be a necessary means in certain situations for extending democracy on a global basis, or is such an aspiration ruled out by the great-power interests necessarily involved in that process? The imposition of democracy or its construction 'from outside' is in deep tension with the democratic idea itself. Much of the violence in contemporary politics stems from its paradoxical association with the democratic idea. Violence and democracy are intertwined since some liberal-democratic states use violence and war in order to overthrow authoritarian regimes and install democracy. These attempts are counter-productive because installing democracy 'from outside' is a process which breeds further violence. The violent resistance stimulated by such democracy-building projects involves themes of resistance to outside oppression, itself one of the chief forms of violence in contemporary politics. The empirical difficulty and the theoretical contradictions involved in forcing democracy on to societies which have not been democratic lead to the proliferation of violence rather than its exclusion or to the substitution of forms of democratic politics for the politics of violent confrontation.

Violence in Favour of Democracy: The Case For

This section presents arguments in defence of the use of violence to install or create democracy, arguments which will be evaluated and criticised further on. Looking at global politics in the present conjuncture of world politics, violence in the form of war is evident. The 'war on terror' was presented in more positive form as a war *for* democracy, and justified in both positive and negative terms. Negatively, it was defended as a necessary response to attacks such as those of 9/11 and to the undoubted existence of global movements whose avowed aim is to combat democracy in all its forms, seen as a system based on false secular foundations with which there can be no compromise. Therefore such movements have to be fought by violent means and through violence exercised by states. No democratic dialogue or compromise is possible with movements which do not seek inclusion in the democratic system or recognition for their particular identity, since their ultimate aim is the destruction of democracy through attacks on the security of citizens of democratic societies. What is argued for in this perspective is not just that the response has to involve violence, but that the agents of that response should be states and their armies or other counter-terrorist forces. States are seen as the only effective force against such a challenge, precisely because it is the central task of the liberal-democratic state to protect and guarantee the security of its citizens. In other words, the monopoly of violence held by such a state is legitimated when it is deployed correctly to repel attacks on the democratic way of life of its citizens.

Such is the negative justification for violence exercised by states in a global context – negative in the sense being of a reaction against a hostile non-state force or movement which challenges democratic societies and their way of life. However, violence in the service of spreading democracy is defended in a more positive sense. The claim is made that a democratic world would be a more peaceful world where violence on a global scale would diminish, since the spread of democracy gives more opportunity for interests and conflicts to be addressed through the channels of peaceful reconciliation and compromise. Therefore violence is necessary as a means to remove non-democratic regimes so that in the aftermath the peaceful reconciliation of conflict is more likely than before. Again the question arises as to the agencies and forces through which such processes of democratisation are to be carried out. What is involved here is a process of democratisation from outside, since societies such as Iraq or Afghanistan have been hitherto ruled by authoritarian non-democratic forces whose grip on power has made impossible the self-rule of the citizens of those societies. This argument ignores the *Realpolitik* of great-power interests and seeks to portray intervention for democracy in the best possible light, since the aim is to suggest how those who advocate the spreading of democracy world-wide propose the use of state violence to that end. It is viewed as doing for other societies or for their citizens what they themselves are unable to do because of the oppressive nature of previous regimes and forms of rule.

Foreign intervention by violent means is thus viewed as a means of transition, hopefully brief, to self-rule by the citizens of those societies, a self-rule which has not been possible in the past. The assumption underlying such arguments is strong in the sense that it assumes that all human beings have an interest in ruling themselves rather than being dominated by power-holders who are not checked and controlled by those over whom they rule. In other words, the assumption of democracy as a universal value rests on a particular view of human beings as willing autonomy rather than domination. And they are seen as being capable of exercising such autonomy if given the opportunity of doing so, of developing and extending their capacities in democratic skills of self-government. Clearly the calculus of violent foreign intervention has to weigh up a number of factors. In the first place, the case in favour rests on the assumption that the potential democrats or active citizens of the country to be liberated are unable to achieve their liberation and democratic enfranchisement for themselves in the present or foreseeable future. There is thus a calculus of a cost-benefit kind, which would treat the gains of present intervention to secure democratic rights as outweighing the unavoidable costs of doing so. Those costs come in terms of both human lives and infringements of democratic principles themselves. If democracy is about self-rule and autonomy, is intervention by some outside force itself compatible with these principles? Such principles seek to forbid or at least to minimise paternalistic actions which take political activity out of the hands of those who as democratic citizens are supposed to be their own rulers. The defence of democratic intervention by violent means rests on an assumption that such intervention will be both temporary and effective. Effectiveness is here understood as requiring the quick destruction of those institutions and structures which impede the self-rule of citizens in the society in question, and equally importantly the construction of a functioning state capable of guaranteeing the stability of the institutions needed for democratic politics. Without an effective state able to protect citizens and guarantee their rights to cooperate on equal terms, a new democracy could not begin to operate.

In the contemporary conditions of world politics violence and democracy thus go hand in hand in the sense that violence has been used by states (in the present conjuncture notably the USA) to spread democracy. The justification for state violence has been that it is employed as a necessary measure to eradicate obstacles to the self-rule of citizens of a particular country, when those citizens have been unable to rule themselves because of authoritarian structures. The export of democracy, if necessary through violent means, is therefore presented in terms of democratic norms and values themselves, both in the negative sense of the removal of obstacles and in the positive sense of the creation of a state form which promotes and enables democracy in the country concerned. This process is seen as stemming from both state-related national interests, securing liberal-democratic states against violent attacks, and from altruistic concerns, enabling people in the liberated country to enjoy the democratic rights which the authoritarian structures of the past have obstructed.

If this case is accepted, then violent actions carried out by liberal-democratic states are necessary and justifiable as means to the end of fostering a less violent and more democratic world. It would therefore be the case that violence arises necessarily in reaction to the challenge of anti-democratic movements which themselves operate on a global level. More positively, such violent intervention encourages democratic practices and in the foreseeable future reduces the recourse to political violence in the world at large, since more democracy means less violence.

Problems of Using Violence for Democracy

Yet these justifications are all problematic, both in theoretical terms and in terms of their basis in experience. Democracy involves as its core value the idea of self-rule. It is therefore incompatible with the idea of such a system being brought into being by forces or agencies other than those who are to be the citizens of a self-governing society. The idea of democracy being created from outside the potentially self-governing society thus contains within itself a contradiction (Beetham 2009). It involves an idea of paternalism or heteronomy on the part of the democracy-creating or democracy-bringing agency supposed to empower the citizens who subsequently develop the capacity to rule themselves. In terms of classical political theory, this evokes Rousseau's discussion in *The Social Contract* of the role of the legislator. The legislator sets up the mechanisms of democratic self-rule and then, according to Rousseau, gracefully retires from the scene, having achieved the goal of stimulating people to become citizens and creating the institutions enabling them to behave as such (Rousseau 1968 [1762]). Yet this disposes too easily of the tension between the democracy-creating role and the particular interests of the agency which creates that democracy. In Rousseau's perspective, the legislator seems to be envisaged as an altruistic individual who is happy to withdraw after the democratic mechanisms have been created. In the real world of contemporary politics, democratic installation through violence has been carried out by states, indeed by certain specific states which possess the necessary strength and military power to perform the task. These states have their own agenda and interests, and the result is therefore that democratic installation through violence is at odds with the democratic aim of self-rule by citizens. The whole project becomes entwined with particular interests and values which may have only a loose connection with democratic values and institutions.

One good example of this is the case of Afghanistan, well described in a recent study as a case of 'democratising a dependent state' (Suhrke 2008). The massive international efforts needed to rebuild the state, develop its economy and restore security all 'eroded the very foundation of democracy as a system in which national representative institutions set priorities, implement policy, and are accountable for the results to its people' (Suhrke 2008: 631). Most of the funds needed for the reconstruction of the state in Afghanistan came from foreign donors. Control of money was not in the hands of the newly created parliament, but mainly in the hands of the donors (the international forces) who were negotiating with the executive power in Afghanistan. Suhrke sums up the situation well, with regard to the weakness of parliament (at the time of writing) in post-Taliban Afghanistan: 'In a stroke of irony, the international community has promoted democratisation but simultaneously created a state so dependent on external support that it deprives the critical institution of liberal democracy, the legislature, of its meaning' (Suhrke 2008: 645).

Furthermore, again following Suhrke, the project of democratisation was imposed from outside by means of war. Yet in the aftermath of war, creating democracy was only one among other aims, and in all probability not the chief consideration: 'democratic reform assistance was a part of a much broader and increasingly controversial international presence that grated on Afghan nationalist sensibilities' (Suhrke 2008: 634). The interests of the 'democracy-imposing forces' lay more in security than democracy, and predominantly in fighting the Taliban because they had sheltered Al Qaeda, rather than in a disinterested fostering of the values of democracy. This then led to inclusion of a number of groups and individuals in the process of political transformation whose democratic credentials were rather dubious, but who had been effective allies in the war against the Taliban. It was also the case that the way in which the institutions of democracy were created 'suited Washington's primary policy objective in Afghanistan, which was not to promote political democracy but to eliminate terrorists and Al Qaeda' (Suhrke 2008: 641). The creation of the post-Taliban regime in Afghanistan resulted in a presidential system rather than a mixed system with a prime minister, presumably because such a presidential system made it easier for the international forces to transmit their policies and to have a single interlocutor with whom they could have effective exchanges, rather than be engaged in a complex situation of democratic negotiation and bargaining. The same factors explain the creation of a weak parliament rather than one structured with well-organised parties and with effective power.

Suhrke's article shows well the complexities and difficulties of creating democracy in the aftermath of war and violence. The fact of international financial superiority and military power, along with the mixture of demands for security and concern for the interests of the intervening states, suggest that the installation of democracy by violent means in the aftermath of violent conflict is a highly problematic exercise which in fundamental ways goes against core democratic values.

Violence as a Global Challenge

This then leads on to the more general question of globalisation and violence, which has to be tackled in any study of the issues. The above section dealt with state-sponsored violence on an international scale, with dominant states using violence and war as means of spreading democracy. However, one has to confront the question of whether it is globalisation itself as a process which stimulates violence, and the implications of this for democratic politics. The line of analysis here is to suggest that democracy is challenged by globalisation in new ways which arise from the very processes of globalisation themselves. Globalisation is the cause of new forms of violence which themselves make the future of democracy more problematic on a world-wide scale. The following analysis seeks to explain the ways in which globalisation creates distinct forms of violence carried out both by state and non-state actors, and how this presents a set of challenges or problems for democratic systems. Such challenges are new and hence require responses in terms of institutions and ideas which so far have not emerged from the politics of liberal-democratic societies.

What then are these new forms of violence emerging as a result of the processes of globalisation? And how should democratic societies respond to them? It is necessary to show the ways in which on an international level globalisation provokes violence and the challenges which this raises for democratic politics both within and beyond particular states. Because of the internationalisation of politics, both state and non-state actors behave in ways which utilise violent means for political ends, even if (in some cases) democracy is proclaimed to be the goal those violent actions are meant to achieve. Hence the use of violence proliferates and in turn creates more violent counter-responses, so that the democratic aim of channelling conflict into peaceful processes is made more problematic.

This raises the question of the new forms of war taken in contemporary politics. With the aim of spreading democracy world-wide comes the question of the means needed to do this. The contemporary insistence on democracy, understood as liberal-democracy in a market or capitalist setting and seen as a universally desirable system, means that the temptation to impose it by force is heightened, especially where the political means and will to do so are available. Thus the globalisation of politics involves concentration on a particular model of democracy and the willingness to impose this, at least in certain cases, through violence or war. The agencies of such political and supposedly humanitarian intervention are states, or at least those states, and particularly the United States, which possess the military capacity and political will to intervene for the purposes of imposing democracy world-wide. However, this in turn invites reaction on the part of those who perceive this project of spreading democracy world-wide as fundamentally flawed, for various reasons. The shape of world politics has changed as a result of globalisation and this has encouraged the resort to violence on the part of both state actors and in the response of non-state movements opposing the imposition of a particular version of democracy. The attempt to spread democracy leads to a more violent world. The project of defending and spreading democracy has become caught up with more particular aims, linked to the interests of those states who propose themselves as the agents of democracy promotion. A particular model of democracy associated with market relations and with a particular form of culture, associated with the American and Western world generally, is presented as a universal and generally applicable model. The chief examples of this process are clearly the interventions in Iraq and Afghanistan, where attempts to create democracy have been moulded by the weight of the process coming from outside, from international agencies superior in wealth and military power as compared with the citizens of the societies to which they were supposedly bringing democracy. Beyond such limitations, however, the imposition of democracy through violence has in these cases done little to create the kind of effective state and associative civil society that are necessary features of a healthy democracy. These are not institutions which can easily be created from above or from outside. This leads to scepticism over the project of creating democracy through any direct intervention. The attempt to do so sparks off an 'equal and opposite' reaction in terms of violent movements which see the imposition of democracy as a form of attempted foreign domination which should be resisted on nationalist grounds. Such resistance to outside domination combines a number of factors. In Iraq, for example, resistance to the supposed democratisation included both a rejection of democratic ideals as incompatible with local beliefs as well as a protest against the exclusion of formerly powerful Sunni groups from participation in political power. Perhaps most powerful of all has been a resistance to the whole process of engineering democracy as something imposed from outside the country and as hence an illegitimate project.

States and Violence: Action and Reaction

These arguments need to be developed in further detail, in order to show the complex relationship between globalisation, violence and democracy. The interrelationship between these three factors suggests that the attempt of the nation-state to exercise a monopoly over the means of violence is more problematic in the conditions of contemporary politics, with the implication that the framework for any possible solution to the problem of violence has to take new forms which go beyond the nation-state. Violence has been globalised or internationalised in ways which require new explanations. The condition of post-Cold War politics is such that the (relative) balance of power between two super-powers has been replaced by a hegemonic United States, whose power is challenged by a host of movements. In this new situation, one model of democracy (liberal-democracy in a market setting) has been proclaimed as the universally valid one. There is, however, a need to distinguish between democracy as a universal value appealing to a need felt by human beings in all places to rule themselves, and particular forms of this universal value marked by historically formed institutions and particular processes, such as those forms which constituted liberal-democracy as it developed in certain societies of Western Europe and North America.

Globalisation can be seen as primarily an economic process, indeed one anticipated by Marx and Engels in *The Communist Manifesto* with the idea of a world market bringing all societies under its sway and sweeping away traditional institutions which seek to hold back this process. Marx and Engels saw the process of capitalist globalisation (though of course they did not use the word) as one in which 'all that is solid melts into air', i.e. traditional social and political institutions whose legitimacy rests on history and veneration of the past come to be seen as irrelevant to a new capitalist order which is contemptuous of tradition (Marx and Engels 1973 [1848]). The process of globalisation in its contemporary form can be seen in a similar way, as undermining those institutions based on the nation-state whose aim was to achieve a degree of solidarity between citizens and provide a minimum of security against the ravages of the market. From this follow some of the problems of social-democracy in the conditions of modern politics, since it was precisely the task of social-democracy to contain the market, to subordinate 'markets' to 'politics' (Esping-Andersen 1985).

If globalisation is in the first instance an economic process which reduces the security of those subject to its dynamism, it has as a corollary a particular model of democracy, defined here as liberal-democracy in a strong market setting. This model has been presented as a world-wide necessity, a kind of precondition for states wishing to enter the modern community of nations or to be considered a legitimate recipient of financial aid and political support from dominant states. It has been imposed world-wide, in certain places through violence, and through the agencies of dominant states and key institutions of politico-economic respectability which act as disciplinary agents of the system. This analysis has much in common with the so-called neo-Gramscian theories developed by writers like Robert Cox (1993). Cox analyses the disciplinary effect of key institutions of this new world order, which seek to regulate societies world-wide in the name of a financial orthodoxy and a new common-sense deemed necessary for social stability. Certain processes are 'locked in' to this global system, while others are excluded or 'locked out' (Gill 1993). The result of this disciplinary power of certain key institutions and dominant states is that one model of democracy is seen as the only legitimate one. Democracy thus becomes in certain conditions associated with violence, where dominant states or a coalition of such states are able to overthrow an authoritarian regime (as was the case with Iraq) and seek to build up a particular form of democracy, namely the hegemonic one sketched out and defined here as a liberal-democratic system in a strong market context. Such a process is seen as necessary both for the security of these dominant states and as valuable in its own right.

The imposition of such a form of democracy, seen as beneficial on a global or world-wide level, has consequences which promote violence in a number of ways. On the part of those imposing democracy, it leads to the association of democracy with great-power interests and with a certain culture, and raises the problem of the agencies of democratisation. If the forces which bring this model of democracy to the global stage are associated with particular states and a particular cultural pattern, this then stimulates violence in two contrasting ways. On the part of the supposedly 'democracy-creating' agents, it presupposes that the project of spreading democracy is a legitimate one which can if necessary justify violence on an international scale. There are a number of problems raised by this supposed democratic internationalism. The project of democratisation is closely tied up with particular great-power interests, notably those of the United

States. Democratisation is seen as a project that does not shrink from violent means because what is at issue is the more peaceful world which would emerge if this particular form of democracy were more widely spread. This involves new forms of war. These new forms of war are global wars which seek to spread democracy on a global level, and which see the sphere of action as correspondingly international and world-wide in scope. As noted by the editors of a recent survey of *Globalisation and Violence*: 'Humanitarian intervention is associated with a dominant and global ideological projection around the notions of "democracy" and "freedom."' They further argue that 'The embodiment of democracy implies a moralisation of politics, a dichotomisation between the evil and dangerous and the democratic and good. This supplies a rationale for war in which bombing for peace becomes a principal strategy' (James and Friedman 2006: xxiii).

Global wars are thus justified on the part of the dominant powers as bringing democracy in a particular format to those societies lacking it and thereby contributing to this 'moralisation of politics' which changes the nature of war. If war is waged on a global scale in the name of democracy in such terms, then violence becomes both justified and more likely as a necessary tool employed in the real world. It is seen as needed in order to secure democratic rights for people around the world. Such justifications widen the scope for violence and war. In a more restricted and traditional sense, war was resorted to when a society or nation needed to defend its independence and right to exist against an aggressive enemy. By contrast the idea of spreading democracy through the actions of leading states extends the range of reasons by which war and state violence can supposedly be justified. Hence the category of global war waged to impose a form of democracy in more proactive or pre-emptive ways licenses violence for purposes other than strict self-defence or the maintenance of a particular way of life.

The result is paradoxical in a number of ways: the worldwide spread of democratisation has resulted in greater violence carried out in its name. Violence is now deemed legitimate on an international scale in the name of humanitarian intervention and the spreading of democratic values. This leads to oppositional movements whose counter-violence is in its turn inspired by the notion of resistance to the very project of imposing a form of rule from outside the society concerned. Thus the new world of global imposition of democracy from outside comes up against movements who in their turn use violence with equal democratic legitimacy. They claim to be acting in the name of 'the people' who resist foreign state powers acting to impose a system declared to be of fundamental and universal significance.

Violence as Resistance to Democratic Imposition

The globalisation of politics thus leads to an extension of violence, since the limits which previously restrained the use of violence have been exceeded in contemporary conditions. If war in the classical conditions of the Westphalian model of the state was envisaged for reasons of *Realpolitik* – in other words in defence of the interests of the state – in contemporary conditions war and violence are contemplated for other and broader reasons, though these do not exclude defence of the state's interests. The idea has become widespread that one form of democratic politics is alone legitimate, and that such a form involves the formal institutions of liberal-democratic politics within the framework of a market economy and a generalised 'Western' culture. If this is seen as the only acceptable framework for a society, then the imposition of such a model of democracy from outside is seen as a legitimate cause for war, or for the use of violence in selected cases. The criteria for selection are complex, and have to do with the interests of particular states, the degree to which public opinion can be aroused in support of the imposition of democracy from outside, and more practical questions of military effectiveness and contingency. Because of the globalisation of politics, and the end of the Cold War era with its balance of super-powers, the use of violence in the name of democracy has been extended. The project of spreading democracy opens up a broad legitimation for the use of state-led violence (violence carried out by state actors, directly or under their sponsorship). This was not conceivable in a world of nation-states on the Westphalian model, where state violence in the form of war was exercised for more restricted causes, and couched in terms of defence of state interests narrowly conceived. The combination of democracy and globalisation, two dominant features of the present age, has thus widened rather than narrowed the sphere of political violence. This would seem then to contradict the leitmotif of the present work, which insists that democracy and violence are theoretically mutually exclusive, since the extension of democracy involves the inclusion of all voices and interests, thus reducing or even eliminating the necessity of any recourse to violence in order to satisfy grievances or draw attention to neglected identities.

The apparent paradox can be resolved by suggesting that democracy when realised does indeed include dissenting voices. However, the forcible imposition of democracy or the attempt to achieve this not only involves violence on the part of states, but furthermore sparks off a range of resistance movements which may themselves use the language of democracy to justify their own use of violence. It is not merely the forcible or attempted imposition of one form of democracy that stimulates the spread of violence as a political weapon. More generally the spread of market-dominated forms of existence as a result of globalisation creates insecurity for which violence appears a suitable remedy. Attempts to secure human rights on a global level are dependent on particular agents, predominantly highly powerful states, notably the United States. While one model for the spread of democracy and human rights might be developed on the basis of new agencies of cosmopolitan democracy (Archibugi 2008), this has not in fact been realised in the world in which we live. In the actual conditions of contemporary politics, so-called 'humanitarian intervention' has been practised by coalitions of highly powerful states. The resulting imposition of democracy is associated with their particular interests and legitimated by the idea that one form of democracy alone is acceptable, one compatible with an economic framework of free-flowing global exchanges of goods and capital. Hence these forms of democratic imposition carried out on a global level have failed to create a situation of democratic inclusion of voices leading to the ending of violence. On the contrary, they have provoked a range of oppositional movements which use the language of democracy themselves, often associated with nationalist ideas of autonomy and self-determination. Such movements resist by violent means the spreading of a particular culture, way of life and political system, and they do so in the name of identity and authenticity.

Among these oppositional groups it is important to make distinctions between network movements like Al Qaeda, which proclaim their outright opposition to ideas of Western (or any other) democracy, and much more fragmented movements of opposition to currents of globalisation and Western-style democracy. These movements, like the Taliban in Afghanistan, are also no friends of democracy, which they oppose because of its secular nature. Nevertheless, they are able to employ ideas of nationalist resistance to imperialist or foreign domination. Globalisation has weakened the nation-state which functioned as the framework for democracy and democratic rights in an earlier age. In its place two wider structures have arisen. One is a coalition of dominant or hegemonic states which at least in some cases do not shrink from the use of violence as a means of spreading their version of democracy on a global scale. The other is a disparate collection of movements of resistance which also employ violence as a means of political action. The latter is highly heterogeneous, and in most cases the movements which comprise this disparate collection do not aim at anything that could be called democracy. They are exemplified by movements such as those opposing the invasion of Iraq, as well as those in Afghanistan, and also movements of a more classically nationalist kind which appeal to a global public opinion in order to secure their demands. Since communication and the media have long spread beyond the bounds of the nation-state, there is a global public space and a trans-national community to which appeals can be made through the demonstrative use of political violence. This provides further evidence that globalisation and violence go hand in hand, since the expanded space of the political community creates more incentive for a 'demonstration' effect of political violence on a global scale. This demonstration effect is only possible when there is a global community of public opinion, on which acts of violence can have any impact. If communication is restricted primarily to the 'imagined community' of the nation, then this limits the effect of political violence to members of that national community. Acts of political violence then attract less attention and bring the grievance to a narrower audience. The global scale of communication provides an incentive for acts of political violence since violence is in part stimulated by a desire to attract attention to grievances and issues which are not addressed, or perceived as not being addressed, by the 'normal channels' of political institutions. Perhaps the most striking illustration of this is the events of 9/11, which impacted on a global consciousness through the symbolism of the targets chosen and the instant diffusion of images of the attacks through the mass media on a global scale.

Globalisation has thus in some respects intensified the incentives for the recourse to violence as a political weapon. This is in part due to the emphasis on one model of democracy and the market, themselves seen as inseparable, and the willingness to spread and in some cases impose that particular model of democracy world-wide. This in turn encourages a number of oppositional movements which often invoke democracy, though with highly dubious credentials, as a justification for political violence, seen as resistance to this hegemonic spread of a supposedly universal model of democracy. Examples of such resistance in Iraq and Afghanistan are problematic because their relationship to democracy is questionable. The Taliban, for instance, explicitly reject democracy in favour of strict Islamic rule. It might be better to use categories of 'resistance' or 'anti-imperialism' to categorise such movements. They do not necessarily seek democracy, yet they use violence as a means of resistance against what are seen as invading forces seeking to impose a distinctive cultural and political model of 'Western democracy'. The extension of politics on a global scale thus brings with it a greater likelihood of political violence, so that globalisation fosters violence, despite the arguments of those who maintain that a globalised world is a more peaceful one, precisely because of the spread of flows of trade and economic exchanges. The 'network society' (Castells 1996) with its global means of communication creates a larger political community as witnesses to acts of violence. This can increase the incentive to use violence in order to draw attention to situations of exclusion, marginalisation and lack of access to the established channels of political power. Finally, movements of protest and nationalist resistance employ acts of violence as a political weapon. Violence is used both as a means of appealing to a world-wide public opinion and also to express a political discourse which contains themes of anti-imperialist or anti-colonial resistance, echoing the ideas of democratic theory, even if in a distorted way. If democracy requires a community in which every participant is recognised as a legitimate interlocutor, no such community exists at present at the international level.

The solution to these problems, the means of achieving the democratic exclusion of violence, has to be sought on a global scale with the achievement of new forms of political community. Violence can only be steered into democratic channels by new institutions which can include those hitherto excluded. While the final chapter of this book seeks to develop the full implications of these 'solutions' to the problem of violence on an international level, some preliminary arguments can be outlined here. It is clear that violence can never be completely eradicated from politics on a national or international level, and that liberal-democratic states remain the agents for meeting the challenge of violence. At the same time the danger persists that the use of violence by states, whether liberal-democratic or not, can escape democratic control and result in the escalation of violence to the detriment of democratic politics.

The problem of globalisation and violence arises because the requirements of democratic community are far from being met on an international or global scale. The problem is thus more intractable on this global level than on the national scale. The reason for this is the absence of community on an international level, a community through which the issues that lead to conflict could be resolved through democratic institutions and procedures of compromise and conciliation. Violence occurs when identities are not recognised, or more broadly when interests cannot be satisfied through institutional channels of democratic politics. Thus if globalisation intensifies the recourse to violence, the corollary must be that this points to the need to develop institutions on a global level which could provide the channels for reconciliation of conflicts which otherwise might result in violence. This in turn leads to arguments developed by those sympathetic to themes of cosmopolitan democracy, or what is called the 'global community of citizens' (Archibugi 2008). What is envisaged are institutions working on a global level which would provide structures to include those who are marginalised and have inadequate 'voice' in conditions of contemporary politics. This would entail a move away from great-power politics in which dominant or hegemonic states have the overwhelming capacity to decide where and when to make so-called 'humanitarian interventions'. It would also require the creation of forums of international politics which bring into a deliberative ambit a wider range of voices than those of dominant states, or even of state powers which are not so dominant. Forums of an international kind could involve civil society groups and could reach out to those who might otherwise resort to violence as a means of expressing their interests or articulating their resentment at their exclusion from effective power-influencing politics.

The line of argument here follows the attempt by Archibugi to expound the idea of a global community of citizens, on the analogy of Schnapper's concept of the nation-state as bringing together citizens in a national community irrespective of ethnic origin or personal belief (Archibugi 2008; Schnapper 1994). The nation-state sought to regulate violence and to substitute dialogue for violent conflict, and in the period of modernity it did so relatively successfully. However, while containing violence within its boundaries, the nation-state 'exported' violence through the phenomena of colonialism and imperialism. Western nation-states imposed their economic demands and their military and political power on the colonies which they appropriated. In the post-colonial situation, the structure of economic power created on a global scale has subordinated the former colonial states and undermined their aspiration to combine national liberation with economic development.

In the contemporary world the 'taming' of the violence induced or fostered by globalisation can only come about through the development of new institutions capable of tackling the question of violence on a global level in the same way that, in a previous historical epoch, the nation-state regulated the question of violence within a national framework. The nation-state contributed to the 'civilising process' (Elias 1978) in which, over the course of time, dialogue took precedence over fighting as a means of resolving conflict. The new institutions of cosmopolitan democracy would aspire to create some kind of global community in which such dialogue could take place. They would aim to include what are conventionally called civil society groups as well as states with their military apparatus and political structures. It is clear that this is an optimistic scenario which presents considerable difficulties and needs further argument if it is not to appear 'utopian', in the sense of a beautiful but unrealisable dream. How can global wars be prevented, if, as argued above, the processes of globalisation themselves arouse a wider range of resistance and opposition? In addition, the problem is deepened because of the weaker power of the nation-state, the agent historically responsible for containing and avoiding violence. The solution, as noted in the previous chapter, lies in what Habermas (Habermas 2001) calls a '*Schliessung*', or closure at the international level to achieve an equivalent degree of containment of violence to that achieved by the nation-state, but without the 'collateral damage' inflicted by the nation-states with their colonial and imperialist policies in the period from 1870 to our own day.

One problem with this perspective is that the power of the state, especially that of dominant or would-be hegemonic states, is not going to disappear. Similarly, it is unrealistic to expect the disappearance of globalisation and of the organisations and structures which 'lock in' (Gill 1993) various disciplinary forces constraining citizens and governments to act in certain ways which reinforce the system itself. Globalisation is often presented as a process of peaceful economic and cultural exchange, the extension of which will result in the spread of democracy and hence reduce the likelihood of violence at an international or global level. In this respect the argument bears some resemblance to the thesis of 'ultra-imperialism' developed in the period before the First World War by (among others) the chief representative of orthodox Marxism, Karl Kautsky (Geary 1987: 55). That thesis held that war would be less likely precisely because of the increasing nexus of economic and commercial contacts throughout the world, and because of the aversion of the bourgeois class to any war or violent action which might disrupt such profitable commercial exchanges. However, the view of globalisation presented here takes a less sanguine perspective, since it holds that globalisation excludes as much as it includes, in the sense that it imposes a kind of 'iron cage' on political actors, states and governments as well as citizens, throughout the world. Such exclusion, as we have seen, is a potent factor in stimulating the recourse to violence. Those who are excluded are tempted to resort to violence since the established channels of global political institutions appear to offer no chance of providing recognition of identity or of responding to grievances or demands.

While it might appear naïve to talk of a definitive solution to such problems, the response cannot be to wish away the forces of globalisation, even though such a globalised world creates more agents of violence. The nation-state attempted, classically, to achieve the monopoly of violence of which Max Weber spoke (Weber 1970 [1919]), and in its heyday managed this with a fair degree of success. In contrast, the processes of globalisation result in a proliferation of groups and agents of violence, however small in size some of them might be. Particular groups express movements of resistance, some of which, like the Palestinian resistance against Israeli dominance, have world-wide consequences and implications. If the solution cannot be to hope for the disappearance of globalisation or to expect that the nation-state on its own can maintain its monopoly of violence, then alternative perspectives have to be found to develop the democratic community on a global level. These could take some of the forms indicated by theorists of cosmopolitan democracy, who envisage a reformed United Nations as one possible structure for achieving a degree of community on the international level which is lacking at the moment.

We can conclude this chapter by returning to the observation that underlies Bobbitt's study (Bobbitt 2008), to the effect that terrorism operates in a global way as a response to the new kind of state which has replaced the nation-state of the previous epoch. If the nation-state has become a market state, as Bobbitt argues, then violence itself becomes global and imitates the state which it is challenging in its form and in its structures. If the nature of political power and order-maintaining structures have changed from concentrated forms of sovereign power to more diffused structures of power, then these changes are mirrored in movements using violence to challenge the 'order' of the state – whether or not we agree with Bobbitt that the latter can be best described as a 'market state'. Violence and the challenge to democracy which it represents elude control and hence become more difficult to deal with because of their networked character. With networked movements of any kind, movements described as typifying a 'new transnational activism' (Tarrow 2005), there is no 'head', no single directing power which can be attacked or with whom negotiations might be undertaken. In that sense terrorist violence is something of an intractable problem for the governments and citizens of a liberal-democracy to deal with, since the networked or 'rhizomatic' character of such violence makes such movements more elusive.

The other implication is more positive, though still problematic, and relates to the response of liberal-democratic societies to this more amorphous challenge from movements which are not structured in orthodox hierarchical ways like political parties or states. The response of liberal-democratic societies has in its turn to mirror the nature of those movements, by developing both a new political discourse and also new institutions which can respond to the networked character of the groups challenging liberal-democratic societies. The message of the present book is that new strategies need to be evolved to aim at the inclusion of those groups and movements for whom violence is an expression of exclusion and the perception of lack of recognition through established channels. Such a perception and the violence resulting from it has to be met by a political transformation of the institutions and discourses of liberal-democracy, along lines which meet the decentralised nature of its challengers. If violent movements arise as a response to exclusion, and if their amorphous and decentralised character reflect in turn the market-dominated nature of the state, then the response of the state has to be similar: it has to develop a range of institutions through which dialogue with hitherto excluded members of society could be embarked on. This would have to be an alternative to the concentration of power in a single central institution. What is envisaged here is a range of inclusive institutions in the wider civil society, through which democratic community could be rebuilt on new lines. The next chapter deals with one crucial aspect of this process, namely the creation of a common culture of citizenship which could equally well perform the task of civic inclusion.

7 Culture, Violence and Democracy

Culture and Violence

The purpose of this chapter is to advance the argument from a 'diagnosis' of the problem of violence as a challenge to democracy to the question of 'cure', even though these medical metaphors may not be entirely appropriate, since the implication of what has been argued so far is that violence can never be totally eradicated from democratic, or any other, society. Violence is practised by the state to maintain 'order', and it is in certain circumstances used by groups and individuals opposing the state. Such opposition may be the expression of an integral or fundamental enmity towards the ideals and institutions of democracy as such, though more often it is an extreme call for recognition, or a protest against the lack of such recognition. Violence is a challenge to the democratic ideal because it substitutes fear and physical coercion in place of the reasoned argument and compromise which constitute democratic means of resolving conflict. The response of democratic societies to this challenge has to be in terms of ensuring greater inclusion. This deprives those using violence as a political tool of any justification for the necessity of violent action as a means of drawing attention to a 'historic' grievance, such as may be exploited by political entrepreneurs and their followers. Increasing inclusion, however, may not be enough to satisfy those who see democracy as fundamentally illegitimate, and the challenge of such individuals and groups has to be met through violence, controlled and limited by institutions of democratic politics. The more hopeful assumption made here is that this form of the threat to democratic politics can be minimised. This goal would be achieved if those whose marginalisation or lack of recognition lead them to sympathise with the use of violence as a political weapon are able to play a role in the institutions of democratic society, from which in present conditions they are excluded.

Clearly, the problem here is how to achieve this greater degree of inclusion and a stronger feeling of citizenship and common identity, in order to prevent such alienation and disaffection from constituting the bases of violent action. The perspective offered in this chapter focuses on culture, both as the problem and as the solution, or at least part of the solution. Culture is part of the problem because it is the lack of recognition of cultural difference, in the broadest sense, which is one of the main causes of violence. It is when people feel aggrieved in their sense of identity that violence constitutes a mode of expression, a reaction to the lack of recognition which is seen as a problem insoluble except through means of violent antagonism. In this sense culture is a cause of violence. The lack of a common culture which used to be sustained by the liberal-democratic nation-state and which exists in a currently weakened form does not necessarily directly lead to violence, but makes it more difficult for the recourse to violence to be restrained. This has to be related to the circumstances of contemporary politics and the impact of globalisation. The conditions of contemporary politics on a global level have at one and the same time weakened the grip of a common national culture and simultaneously (and paradoxically) heightened the significance of markers of culture and identity which take a more particularistic and fragmented form. Because of the spread of a globalised economy and the nature of relationships in societies where the market is held to be the supreme form of association, the solidarity offered by the 'traditional' nation-state has been weakened, and no longer brings people together in a strong enough form to satisfy their impulses for a shared identity. Since globalisation leads to weaker solidarity it therefore cannot satisfy the demand for community. This demand surfaces in much more fissiparous and fragmented forms, in the affirmation of distinct identities which are marked, as are all identities, by symbols and ways of life expressed in customs and styles of dress and other cultural markers.

This is not to suggest an immediate jump from cultural difference to violent conflict, with the latter as the necessary and immediate consequence of the former. However, to revert to the basic antithesis of conflict and community, the implications are as follows. If community is needed in order to redirect violent tensions into channels of peaceful recognition, then such an antidote to violence is far more difficult to achieve in the circumstances of contemporary politics. Again, it should be emphasised that this is a matter of degree and does not imply the immediate and total break-up of forms of national solidarity. Nor does it suggest that the weakening of national solidarity is synonymous with violence, or that the decline of a national common culture leads immediately to physical conflicts between different cultural and other groups coexisting in the same national terrain. However, it involves the question of how adequate are the forces which could contain conflict and which might lead opposing groups and individuals to identify with each other to the extent of engaging in shared dialogue and mutual recognition. On the 'community' side of the equation then, there is to be noted a deficit in the 'violence restraining' features which steer conflict away from violent confrontation and stimulate peaceful reconciliation. This in turn suggests the need to investigate whether there could be, in today's conditions, the development, creation or even re-creation of a common political culture which would perform this function of diminishing the temptation to have recourse to violence as a means of expressing the conflicts inherent in any complex society.

It is in that sense that culture could form one element of the 'solution' (partial though that might be) to the problem of the challenge of violence to democratic institutions. Yet at the same time the problem is deepened because culture is also part of the problem, which makes any solution harder to achieve. If community is a far weaker force because of a decreased degree of solidarity on the national level, conflict is a more potent force. The reason for this, however, is not just the decline of community, as though a lower degree of community automatically entails a higher degree of conflict in a simple proportional reaction. The more significant factor is the 'cultural turn', which imbues conflict or difference with a cultural dimension which makes democratic reconciliation and compromise more difficult to achieve. Conflicts over identity and culture are not such as lend themselves to solutions of a 'split the difference' kind. These are forms of conflict where common ground is less likely to be found. Therefore the temptation to resort to violence as a means of political expression is greater, unless contained within a shared framework of reference which permits and encourages dialogue and mutual respect for interlocutors as equally entitled citizens. Yet this common framework is made more difficult by the changed nature of conflict in contemporary politics and by the decline of community.

Culture is thus likely both to provoke violence as well as to offer a way out of violent conflict. The former is true because of the quite fundamental role that culture plays in identifying who we are, and in offering a key to the problem of personal identity. Thus aggrieved identities are the ones most likely to explode into violence, since the failure to extend recognition and acceptance to certain groups or individuals weakens any reason they might have for abiding by shared procedures and democratic dialogue. Hence the fundamental idea is for citizens to recognise each other as members of a common democratic association. This is necessary for a democratic society to function as a means of containing conflict. However, cultural diversity runs the risk of heightening barriers to such a shared democratic consciousness to the point of violent conflict, if distinct and separate cultural groups are imbued with a feeling that their particular culture has no recognition or right of existence in the wider society. This is why nationalist conflicts are especially hard to channel into processes of democratic politics because they raise the most fundamental issues concerning the composition and membership of the democratic association. Conflict, inherent in any complex society, can only be dealt with in a non-violent way if the potential actors accept legitimate means, other than violent ones, of dealing with the issues out of which conflict arises. Those issues are primarily ones of nationalism, religion and social deprivation. It is clear that the first two of these categories are cultural, providing a key to people's identity and sense of who they are. The conflicts arising out of these issues are the hardest to resolve, since they involve patterns and styles of life as well as (in the case of nationalism) the demand for a degree of political autonomy and a set of political institutions which will provide for defence of the culture in question. Alain Touraine's question 'can we live together?' (Touraine 2000) is a pertinent one here: can different identities, cultures and belief systems live together in the same territory and under the same state without falling into patterns of violent conflict when each group or culture demands a state of its own (or at the least a degree of political autonomy) as the necessary condition for recognition and defence of its identity?

It is in such ways that culture can be the basis for violent antagonism, and that Touraine's question has been answered in the negative, especially in conditions where democratic institutions have been either absent or present only in weak form. The examples of genocide in the modern world, for instance the ethnic conflicts and massacres in Rwanda, provide extreme cases of a scenario where distinct groups have *not* been able to coexist peacefully and where violence destroyed, for some considerable time, the possibility of a common democratic community. But even where democratic institutions are implanted to a greater degree than they were in this case, democratic community is much more problematic where different cultural, national and religious groups share the same territory and the same state, and where the temptation to resort to secessionist separation remains a permanent possibility. Examples here range from Lebanon with its range of religious and ethnic groups, to Belgium with the two cultures of Walloon and Flemish national groups coexisting with less than total harmony in the same state, and indeed to all contemporary liberal-democracies where a range of cultural and ethnic groups exist and make demands for recognition on a state historically dominated by a particular ethnic and cultural majority whose cultural dominance is now challenged. This poses vast problems for forms of civic republicanism and a political framework within which citizens might share a common democratic allegiance.

If these problems apply to the first two of the three factors listed above as promoting political violence (religion and nationalism), the problem is exacerbated when these 'cultural' features are reinforced by factors of social and economic deprivation, which is frequently the case. Indeed it should be made clear that these three factors are not to be seen as mutually exclusive, and that culture is often allied with social deprivation in a dangerous combination which is likely to fuel violence. If political violence is in many cases the result of a failure of recognition of distinct identities, such failures are frequently associated with a group's inferior status in economic and social terms. This is where the analysis of violence as a call for recognition and inclusion in the democratic community is particularly pertinent, as can be illustrated by the urban riots of 2005 in France, where the protests were a combination of economic grievances with more cultural ones (Muchielli and Le Goaziou 2006). Groups of citizens turned to violent protest in opposition to police brutality, lack of respect and recognition; they opposed a discourse of politics which stigmatised the protestors as a group who should be 'cleansed' rather than included in a circle of civic discourse.

Culture as the Solution for the Problem of Violence

If questions of culture then give rise to political violence, by what means might this challenge of violence be contained? With respect to 'established' liberal-democracies the problem is that of how those tempted to use violence for the reasons indicated above (lack of respect and recognition) could be included in a democratic community where violence is not needed as a means of calling attention to the contested issues. With respect to 'democracies in the making', the problem concerns the establishment of democratic procedures and institutions and the willingness of actual and potential citizens to abandon violence as a means of pursuing their interests. In this case the issue is one of creating a democratic community in which dialogue and compromise are possible. However, in both cases it is a question of developing a common culture in which violence is rejected as a means of political action. The only reason for such a rejection can be that there are other means available for the solution of grievances and political channels through which to secure the respect and recognition due to all citizens. The role of culture in both cases is crucial, though it will form only part of the solution, which has also to involve institutional change, as will be discussed further in the final chapter.

What then is meant by saying that culture could form at least part of the solution to the problem of political violence? The analysis starts from the fundamental idea introduced in our first chapter, that the two elements in democracy are conflict and community. A community in this sense means one which satisfies two requirements: in the first place each of its members has equal status, and is treated by the other members as endowed with an equal right to articulate their point of view and the particular interests which that member wishes to express. In the second place, and as a consequence of the first requirement of equality, the resort to violence is unnecessary in such a democratic community as a means of resolving conflict, since the opportunity exists to engage in dialogue with other members of the community to address grievances and to be included in decisions taken by the community as a whole which affect all its members.

While this is a highly idealised and abstract description of democratic community, it sets out the normative requirements which such a community would have to satisfy. In turn, to be able to function well, all members of the democratic community need to be convinced of the values which hold it together. That is what is to be understood by a culture of democratic community. The question is how such a culture could be created, maintained and instilled in each of its members. The answer to be developed here is situated in the broad framework of a republican perspective. Such a perspective calls for a higher degree of citizen involvement than do liberal-democratic systems as presently constituted, an involvement which succeeds in instilling in its members a belief in some common or public interest and shared commitment to democratic procedures. In the admittedly ideal world here described, resort to physical force and to the politics of violence is rejected both on pragmatic grounds and on grounds of principle as well. How then in more practical terms could existing democracies be reformed or changed so as to realise the aim of reducing the challenge of violence?

The task is made easier when there are shared values which link together the members of the democratic community. In the circumstances of contemporary politics, this is, in contrast, more difficult because of the decline in the homogeneity of the citizen body. This greater heterogeneity together with the insecurity arising out of globalisation set groups of citizens against each other and make cultural difference into an excuse for violence and uneasy relationships between those who should, in ideal terms, regard each other as equal citizens engaged in cooperation within the bounds of democratic community. In particular such tensions arise between those members of the democratic polity who regard the state and the political community as 'theirs' and who reject immigrants and newcomers as not entitled to the rights of citizenship and in particular to the status of equal interlocutors in democratic dialogue. The recent decision taken by referendum in Switzerland to forbid the building of minarets is an unwelcome example of such a case.

There has to be established a culture of common citizenship which functions as an antidote to violence, instead of a situation where certain cultural groups are denied full membership in the democratic community. In the age of nationalism, defined as the period opened up by the American and French Revolutions, it was the democratic nation-state which fulfilled this function with a reasonable degree of success, unifying its citizens and instilling them with a common national culture which combined political unity and a shared history highlighted by shared memories, however myth-like they were. Such a national form of 'imagined community' is not sufficient in the present age to sustain a democratic community robust enough to minimise the challenge of violence. Other bases, global in scope, have to be found, because the nation-state is inevitably marked by a degree of partiality and ethnic identity which impedes its capacity to achieve the community of citizens where violence is rejected as a means of settling conflict. What then could be the bases of democratic community in the contemporary scene, and how could a common culture reduce the risk that people resort to violence?

One reason why the nation-state, at least on its own, is now inadequate as a community to achieve this end of excluding violence is that, as shown in the previous chapter, there are distinct links between globalisation and violence. The challenge of violence has to be understood as occurring on an international level, so that the response has to be equally global or international. However, in the present state of world politics the predominant response to violence has been that of powerful states (notably the USA) acting as the main agent to contain violence through counter-violence, through war and armed force. State violence promotes reaction in terms of counter-violence and fails to come to terms with the underlying reasons which prompt the use of violence as a political weapon. A common culture has to be created on two levels which are not incompatible with each other. The first is the international level, where issues of terrorism and the violence of those excluded from existing international forums could be tackled through a democratic dialogue involving a wider range of actors than the present state-dominated international system. This would involve discussion and negotiation with a wide range of actors, including those who practise terrorism, since such forums would require them to explain and justify their actions. The assumption here is that specified in previous chapters, namely that terrorism and the use of violence generally do not constitute some irrational outburst but involve the use of force for some publicly avowable political end. Hence, a demand for the justification of such use of force is a necessary stage in dealing with political violence.

However, just as on the national level, new institutions would have to be developed to provide forums for these discussions and negotiations. The new institutions would have to include non-state bodies and associations, conventionally referred to as 'civil society' groups, which could form a new or extended public opinion at a global level. It is necessary to defend such proposals against the charge of being naïve and idealistic. It is true (to take one particular example) that one of the issues behind much of the violence in contemporary politics, namely the Israeli-Palestine situation, will not be resolved purely within civil society forums bringing together representatives of the different interests to discuss the issue. It is still states which have the greatest degree of control over the means of violence, and therefore states and their armies and other 'specialists in violence' who will determine any possible solution of the issue.

However, what is envisaged here as a means of minimising the recourse to political violence in contemporary politics is the presence of international forums for dialogue between competing groups, including those who practise violence as a means of securing the ends they wish to achieve. Such international forums would call for statements justifying the use of political violence. Once those statements are made, they can be scrutinised and criticised by other participants in the international forum and, perhaps more importantly, this scrutiny would feed into a debate about international public opinion. In such forums the protagonists of violence could be brought into contact with each other and be made aware of the consequences and implications of their actions. These forums would constitute a means of building up an awareness of the issues in public opinion on an international scale, and hence help put pressure on states to confront the issues giving rise to violence, and on those non-state groups which practise it.

While the focus has changed here from 'culture' to 'institutions', the rationale for this is that it is only through institutional reform (or the creation of new institutions) that what is here called a new culture could be developed. Culture is understood here as a complex of beliefs and assumptions, in this case concerning what is legitimate political action, rather than a more exclusive inward-looking framework of beliefs. The question is one of how those groups and their supporters which practise violence could be induced rather than coerced to renounce the use of violence as a political weapon. This aspiration can only be successful if other means of political action are held open as possibilities, in other words if the potential practitioners of violence see more promising means of pursuing their political ends. In turn, this is only feasible if those practitioners are able to voice their grievances publicly and receive a hearing. This requires the existence of institutions through which such articulation is made possible, so that it can be scrutinised by other parties involved in the discussion and in turn by broader public opinion. Terrorism pays a perverted homage to democracy, since it appeals to a democratic public opinion in order to force a change in that opinion, and thereby generate the impetus for an alteration in policy on the part of governments and states. The road to containing violence lies in altering the perceptions of both citizens and of those engaged in political action concerning the kind of means that are seen as permissible. In other words, what is meant by a change in culture is a change in attitudes to political action, where the aim is to delegitimize the resort to violence as an acceptable or necessary tool for attaining political ends. This can only be achieved if there are institutions and forums through which those political ends can be articulated and confronted and if a broader range of groups and political actors are brought into public discussion than is presently the case. Politics and issues of violence have to be the preserve of a wider public than official state actors. This requires the creation of structures and institutions to accommodate this more inclusive form of politics on an international or global level as well as at the level of the nation-state.

Through being included in these new global institutions, those who might undertake violent actions could be dissuaded from doing so and become convinced of the futility of violence as an effective means of realising political ends. The use of violence by states may be necessary against those who see violence as an end in itself, or who are animated not by the desire for inclusion but by a visceral hostility against democracy itself. However, such movements will not succeed unless they are supported by other citizens who accept the argument that violence is needed to achieve political ends. A culture of non-violence rejects the resort to terrorist or violent means of political action on both practical and moral grounds.

This leaves open for further discussion the question of what would be the common culture needed to underpin such a rejection of violence as a political weapon by the bulk of citizens. Republican theory maintains that it is only through a consciousness of a high degree of common citizenship which transcends cultural divisions that the challenge of violence as a threat to democracy could be met. The republican perspective is the best 'antidote' to the challenge of violence for established liberal-democratic societies. But what exactly would such a republican perspective entail? For a start, it has to be effective in bridging the divisions between sections of the citizen body, divisions which can fuel the recourse to violence for reasons made clear in previous chapters. How could those factors which stimulate violence be overcome so that a more genuine democratic community is created? And if such a model of democratic community is available, in what ways could it be used to facilitate the exclusion of violence from 'democracies in the making', whose democratic transition is threatened if the potential agents of the transition resort to violence instead of accepting democratic procedures of conflict resolution?

The first requirement for a culture of republican common citizenship would have to be that the political institutions of the state in question are not perceived as being permeated by and as perpetuating a dominant majority culture whose assumptions exclude minority groups. This comes up against two obvious difficulties. The nation-state is indeed historically linked to a particular culture with its ethnic and historic roots, so that to envisage a state free from such links is to call for something very different from the nation-state as it exists at the moment. The second difficulty stems from the very fact of cultural diversity within the unit of the nation-state and the consequence that any features of commonality risk being of a very 'thin' kind, too weak to perform the task of civic inclusion needed to preclude the recourse to violence. It is for this reason that some theorists, following Habermas, take the line of 'constitutional patriotism' (Nanz 2006). This suggests that the possession of certain basic rights, enshrined in the constitution or fundamental law, is an adequate basis for the unity of citizens. This is, however, a necessary but not sufficient condition for a culture that would exclude political violence, since living under the same institutions is not on its own adequate to achieve the degree of civic inclusion which would be the best and only effective means of making the resort to violence unacceptable for the majority of citizens. Such constitutional patriotism is part of what a republican concept would involve, but it would need to go further in order that no section of society feels excluded. There has to be a feeling of common belonging stronger than can be provided by constitutional patriotism if violence is to be 'delegitimised' as a possible means of political expression. This is implied by a line of thinking that can be broadly designated as republican, defined in general terms as a perspective which emphasises a membership of a collective political association rather than seeing the polity as the sum total of separate individual interests.

The question of a common democratic culture minimising the recourse to violence has to be understood on the two levels of the global and the national, since violence cannot be adequately grasped solely within the limits of the nation-state. On the international level, new forums need to be developed in which the demands of those exercising political violence can be presented so that the issues fuelling recourse to violence can be understood. This would be the first stage or precondition required as an adequate response to the challenge of violence. On the national level, the idea of a state which guarantees basic rights of the individual irrespective of their cultural or ethnic affiliation is a crucial foundation for the creation of an inclusive political community, but it is not sufficient. The state can no longer be the instrument for propagating one particular culture to which all other groups must subscribe. This would exacerbate the sense of exclusion and victimisation which can trigger the recourse to violence. So a middle way has to be found between on the one hand too minimalist a sense of political community, limited to the mere fact of just living under the same political institutions, and on the other a stifling monolithic culture which denies the diversity of identities and cultures which are an inescapable feature of the contemporary world.

Any solution to the problem of violence has to involve the two core ideas of institutional reform and discursive reform. The underlying idea is to give 'voice' to those whose involvement is at present a very minoritarian one, on the assumption that violence is encouraged if people feel they are not being listened to or included in any effective democratic dialogue. 'Effective' in this context means changing the policies and actions of governments and citizens, rather than introducing mere 'talking shops' from which no policy change might be expected. The concept of institutional reform used here also has to be understood in a wider context. It is not meant to suggest merely the opening up of established institutions to a wider public and to a broader set of constituents. It is meant to propose a more extensive process of the creation of new institutions which could open up new dimensions of that admittedly vague concept of a 'democratic public space' in which new voices or interests presently marginalised could be given a more effective platform from which they might be articulated.

As we have argued in earlier chapters, if political violence is not an irrational outburst or the expression of pathologically disturbed individuals delighting in violence for its own sake, then it is necessary to explain the reasons for the use of political violence as a means of political action. Those reasons differ widely from group to group, but they arise primarily out of cultural issues of failure of recognition stemming from those key features of religion and nationalism. When allied with economic and social deprivation, this presents a powerful 'cocktail' likely to explode in manifestations of political violence. Yet this violence is not irrational, since it aims at a change in the political arrangements of the society in question so that the present arrangements, seen as defective, can be remedied. If that is valid in general terms as a broad explanation of the causes of political violence as practised by non-state groups (although we have seen that violence is practised with equal readiness by states), then this suggests possible strategies for responding to the challenge of violence.

These are not arguments of an ethical kind in which the moral rightness or evil of political violence are assessed. Rather, the arguments presented here seek to understand why people and groups utilise political violence as a means of action, and on the basis of such understanding attempt to point out ways in which a process of democratic reform could change the political calculus of those tempted to use violence. If violence is a sign that all is not well with the democratic system as it presently exists, then the best response is not to meet violence with the organised violence of the state, but to develop the democratic system in such ways as to render unnecessary the use of violence to get one's voice heard. Such a process would show the theoretical incompatibility between democracy and violence, since a 'full' or fully inclusive democracy would provide opportunities for all voices to be heard in ways which (ideally) render violence unnecessary. By the same token, with reference to 'democracies in the making', the attempt to curtail the recourse to violence has to proceed through attempts to involve all members of the polity in agreement on democratic procedures and to allay their fears that they will have no say in the decisions reached by any future democratic order. In both cases, the exclusion of violence can only be achieved through the creation of a shared culture of democratic citizenship. How then can this be developed, and what would it mean for the shape of liberal-democratic politics?

The answer to these questions lies in associating the three ideas of culture, institutional reform and a change in the discourse of politics, with the latter two seen as means to the establishment of a culture excluding or precluding violence. Starting with the idea of institutional reform, the perspective to be defended here suggests that if a process of political and social inclusion is to reduce the recourse to violence, there would need to be fundamental changes in the existing institutions of liberal-democracy, as well as the creation of new institutions. Beyond that, and overlapping with the idea of discursive reform, what is further required is a broader understanding and acceptance, maybe even welcoming, of forms of political action which extend beyond the normal channels of institutional politics, as long as such forms of political action involve attempts at some kind of dialogue with or appeal to other citizens as opposed to forms of violent action which reject such dialogue in favour of fear and coercion. What is involved is a change in the mentality both of those who undertake acts of violence as well as those who are the potential victims of such acts. The perspective developed here suggests that it is not through violence practised by the state that anti-systemic violence can best be met, but through a reconstitution of some of the practices of liberal-democracy at both a national and an international level.

The three facets of institutional reform suggested above, namely reform of existing institutions, creation of new ones, and the acceptance or encouragement of a wider range of political practices, can be explained further as follows. The existing representative institutions in contemporary liberal-democratic societies are for the most part not representative of large sections of society. In their style and social composition they are too restrictive and unappealing to marginalised groups who are in that way excluded from any effective representation through those institutions. This is of course a very sweeping generalisation, and it does not mean to suggest that there are no representatives of disaffected or minority groups in the parliaments or other formal representative institutions of liberal-democratic societies. However, the problem is a deeper one which touches on fundamental problems of democratic societies, namely how to make the representative institutions more inclusive of minority cultural or ethnic groups who risk being alienated by the style, ethos and functioning of political institutions designed for a different social structure. The problem lies with the traditional structures of representative politics which were designed for a different age, in which a centralised representative body with structured parties was an adequate form of representation for a society more unified in its culture or more strictly divided along class lines which were reflected in the representative body. In contemporary liberal-democracies there exists a greater gap between, on the one hand, the formal representative bodies of parliamentary democracies and their political elites, and on the other hand large sections of society and different minority groups whose assumptions and culture are not reflected in the formal representative structures of the society.

Such a disassociation between representative structures and sections of the citizen body does not lead inevitably to political violence. However, the separation of the political class from those who live in the wider society, or from sections of that citizen body, does weaken the effectiveness of the democratic community whose strengthening and reformation would form the best defence against political violence. Hence the implication for political reform would be for political parties in existing liberal-democratic societies to function more effectively as channels for wider participation, rather than merely as vote-getting agencies at election times. This calls for a greater willingness on the citizens of liberal-democracy to involve themselves in the activities of political parties whose 'pulling power' in the present state of things seems low. It may be that this perspective is excessively influenced by recent events in the United Kingdom, where parliamentarians have been tarnished by disclosures of financial scandals concerning their expenses. It would be exaggerated to talk, along with Carl Schmitt (Schmitt 1988), of a 'crisis of parliamentary democracy' to indicate a collapse in the legitimacy of the institutions of representative politics; it is however more defensible to suggest that the relatively restricted nature of the social composition of parliaments and other formal representative bodies is one of the reasons why groups resort to political violence, since they can point to evidence that the existing representative institutions do not reflect their interests or their identities and therefore have no claim on their loyalty. These representative institutions do not provide the channels through which democratic dialogue could be carried out with any hope of meeting the grievances or respecting the identities of broad sections of the citizen body. This indicates the necessity of widening the range of identities represented in these formal institutions of liberal-democratic politics in order to minimise recourse to violence by disaffected groups.

Culture and Community

The obvious question arises as to how this is to be done, and what evidence there might be that increasing the representative range of existing bodies would in fact reduce the risk of political violence. This leads to the second dimension of political or institutional reform mentioned here, the creation of new institutions which would complement the already existing institutions of liberal-democracy. The rationale for such a creation of new institutions is the same as that developed above: the formation of a democratic community requires identification with democratic procedures rather than those of violence, by members of the citizen body. Such identification is facilitated when there are forums through which issues can be raised and identities respected in dialogue with bearers of other identities and cultural affiliations. The decline of working-class solidarities forged in the factory and other such 'Fordist' places of work, so important for Marx and other theorists in the Marxist tradition, has made it more difficult to create a democratic community. The decline of democratic community has in turn eroded barriers to violence because sections of the population are lacking in the broader civic identity which would enable democratic dialogue to replace violence as the means of dealing with conflicts in the wider society. Whereas democratic community was powerfully aided by the integrative institutions of the nation-state and the workplace, both factors are now in a weakened condition. Classical Marxist theory expected the factory to be the locus of class solidarity, overcoming ethnic and cultural difference so that the formation of democratic, indeed socialist, solidarity would render violence unnecessary. Even the socialist revolution would not require violence, since the ever-growing size of the working class and the shrinking dimensions of the class of capitalists would make the latter realise that they could not with any hope of success prevent the victory of their class opponents. Such a perspective is evident in Engels' famous Preface to the re-issue of Marx's *Class Struggles in France*, in which Engels envisaged the progress of the socialist revolution as proceeding with 'the irresistible force of a natural process' (Engels 1973 [1895]: 201). Violence would be unnecessary both from the side of the revolutionaries and futile from the side of that ever-shrinking minority opposed to revolution. Such perspectives are of less relevance in the changed conditions of contemporary politics which give more incentive to those who wish to use violence as a political weapon. The conditions of society are such that they no longer 'automatically', i.e. through their own dynamic, generate the prerequisites of solidarity. This may not necessarily lead to violence but it erodes those links between citizens which would lead them to think of violence as an illegitimate way of articulating interests and of dealing with conflict.

In short, the political institutions of liberal-democracy are no longer adequate, at least in their existing form, for generating the solidarity that would minimise the challenge of violence. This then requires examination of the two further aspects of institutional reform mentioned above, namely, the creation of new institutions and a wider concept of the limits of acceptable political action. With regard to the creation of new institutions, the emphasis here is on the development of forums through which dialogue could take place between bearers of different identities, some of whom could otherwise be led through feelings of resentment and marginalisation to favour violence as a means of political expression. Recognising the inevitability of conflict means paying attention to the need for means to tame that conflict, in other words to find non-violent forms of conflict resolution. From the perspective of democratic theory the emphasis has to fall on the creation of a community of equal citizens among whom dialogue is possible. This is seen (in the present argument) as the best means of responding to the challenge of violence, rather than violent state action. In terms of institutional reform and the creation of new institutions, this would entail the creation of channels through which such democratic dialogue would be possible, whether this would be between citizen groups and state agencies, or communication between such groups in order to foster mutual understanding.

This provides the means for giving content to the idea of a democratic community whose members communicate with each other as a means of resolving differences. It is recognised that such 'jaw jaw' (in Churchill's terms) may not sufficient to prevent the danger of 'war war' (or violent conflict). In particular it does not tackle the insecurity arising on a global level from the spread of neo-liberal market relations and the weakening of the solidarity established formerly by the civic nation-state. Nevertheless, the importance of such democratic dialogue should not be underestimated because it could function as a means of preventing the ghettoisation, or 'encapsulation' into different and separated communities, of the citizen body. In such a case of a divided society, its members have limited communication with each other and this fosters misunderstandings, hostility, resentment and the enclosure of individuals in their private group identity, at the expense of a wider awareness of shared interests as members of a democratic political community. One of the consequences of the fragmentation of class solidarities has been the erosion of an important factor assisting the growth of such a wider sense of association. Since that is the irreversible consequence of fundamental changes in social structure, forms of solidarity which might exclude violence have to be in a sense 'artificially' stimulated by new associations or institutions. The formation of community associations and encouragement of institutions of local representation would bring together citizens and members of different cultural groups and identities in mutual dialogue. Such forums, as already indicated, would involve dialogue between holders of state power and local representatives or members of particular cultural groups. The new institutions envisaged here would also be more horizontal and less vertical in the sense of involving interaction between groups of civil society. The hope would be that such interactions, whether between holders of state power and particular groups (vertical), or between groups of civil society interacting among themselves (horizontal), would induce a degree of citizen solidarity so that violence becomes if not unthinkable then at least less appealing as a means of political expression or articulation of identity.

There has to be some inducement or incentive for people to join such groups. This is one of the problems of a republican-type perspective, since such a perspective assumes a degree of 'civic virtue' in the individual members of a society. Such 'civic virtue' involves a sense of commitment to the public interest and a consciousness of membership of a democratic community. The whole republican perspective thus risks a kind of vicious circle in which a sense of public interest emerges out of participation in civic institutions, but involvement in such institutions is only possible if there is a sense of public interest in the first place. Hence what is to be created is only possible if it already exists in at least embryonic form. If the kind of solidarity which excludes violence is to be achieved through dialogue between groups, which groups are to be involved, and who decides on this? The difficulty arises (often commented on by critics) that seeing this dialogue or attempt at mutual understanding as the product of group interaction risks making identities more solid and fixed. The reason for this would be that such a group-based process privileges a group identity, organised around some concept of a fixed identity which a particular set of people share, whether it be cultural, religious, political or ethnic. The problem here is the obvious one that individuals have a variety of different identities, and if their contribution to resolving the problem of violence is channelled through membership of a group which privileges one particular identity, this runs the risk of congealing individuals within the confines of that single identity.

These problems are not insuperable. The attempt to create forums in which members of different groups would interact with each other functions as an incentive for wider membership, because if they were modestly successful they would be attractive as a forum for articulating issues and explaining the power of certain identities. Perhaps if such institutions were created at a local level with open membership, i.e. with no qualifications or restrictions placed on those who could be members, they could in due course attract a wider membership, so that in that way a wider sense of civic engagement could be created, animated in the first instance by a minority with a heightened sense of public interest, who would draw in after them individuals initially less inclined towards such active participation. The idea here is for an active minority to work through new institutions and encourage others to join them, rather than consider civic virtue as an 'all or nothing' matter possessed either by all or by none. It might be more useful to consider it as a process, something that develops through the pulling power of institutions.

With regard to the problem of giving excessive attention to fixed group identities which place individuals in too rigid categories, this danger could be mitigated by bringing in to the civic circle groups and individuals previously indifferent or even hostile to the possibilities of political engagement held out by the official channels of the state. One example of this in the British context is furnished by Rachel Briggs' study of political activism among British Muslims (Briggs 2010). This shows how forms of political action have been embraced by the younger generation of British Muslims, as opposed to their parents' generation, even if their political activity may take forms which go outside the established channels of more 'respectable' politics. Nevertheless, as Briggs argues convincingly, such forms of political action show a degree of commitment and willingness to be involved in the politics of the British state, or at least in the activity of the wider society.

Such forms of civic activism would thus also suggest a willingness on the part of young Muslims to avoid violence and a readiness to embrace non-violent means of expressing their identity and interests, as well as peaceful ways of drawing attention to their marginalised position within British society. If the idea of a democratic community is to have any relevance, then there has to be acceptance, indeed even a welcoming, of such non-violent but novel forms of political activity, since they constitute evidence of the thesis advanced here that political violence arises when other channels of activity are blocked or non-existent. The three forms of institutional reform focused on here thus in a sense go together. Widening of the opportunities to participate in the existing and 'traditional' representative institutions of the liberal-democratic state should go along with the development of new forums to facilitate civic dialogue between government agents and civil society groups and also between such groups. There should also be acceptance of new forms of political action which may challenge the established institutional framework of the liberal-democratic state but express a desire for civic engagement rather than total rejection of that framework. Taken together, such measures would not only constitute the best antidote to violence as a challenge to liberal-democracy, but would also radically transform the nature of liberal-democracy through changing its institutions. They would transform liberal-democracy in a more 'republican' or civic direction, and thus the goal of a more inclusive democracy would be approximated. Such a transformation would approach the democratic ideal according to which all voices are heard and the recourse to physical force is rejected both on pragmatic grounds as well as on grounds of principle.

Clearly this is in some senses an idealistic aspiration, but the institutional reforms sketched out here, albeit in a necessarily general way, suggest practical means of approaching such a goal. It remains to say something about the second proposed means of responding to the challenge of violence, namely what is here called discursive reform, or a change in the language of politics. This too can be seen as a complement to the institutional reform proposed above. Here the onus would fall on the political leaders and political class of a liberal-democratic society, whereas the impetus for the institutional reform sketched out above would involve more initiatives from the citizens themselves. What is understood by discursive reform is a renewed emphasis by the leaders of democratic society on values of inclusive citizenship and a move away from a language of politics which heightens a sense of marginalisation and 'otherness' on the part of minority groups in society. The discourse of the radical right appeals to the sense of insecurity of groups who formerly felt themselves secure and indeed dominant in 'their' homeland. Such a discourse involves setting up as targets and as scapegoats groups stigmatised as the 'other', whose identity is denounced as 'alien' and as being responsible for the decline of the homeland seen as the exclusive property of the self-proclaimed 'owners' of the nation. This kind of discourse has been the preserve of radical right movements and has fuelled violence against minority groups who are made the target of such violence on the part of those who use them as scapegoats for their own insecurity.

Given that such a discourse exploits insecurity and stimulates violence, it has to be countered by a different language of politics, though of course this is not to suggest that such insecurities can be combated merely through the use of language. However, a new language of politics requires serious attempts by the political leaders of contemporary democracies to establish new bases of inclusive citizenship and to contribute to the forging of democratic political community. This would have to involve not just language but serious policies aimed at citizenship education, at solving problems of immigration and of political refugees. It also has to be made clear that such a new discourse of politics is not something operative only on the level of the nation-state, since it has to be proclaimed at a global level as well. Violence is carried out by people who are desperate for recognition and who see no chance of getting their interests heard through orthodox means of political action. The response then has to be to open up those democratic channels of political action and to develop a new language of politics which contributes to that process and opposes the language of those who target scapegoats and fuel violence in that way. Institutional reform and the development of a new language of politics both provide ways in which democracies can respond to the challenge of violence. Such a response would use that challenge to stimulate and inject new life into liberal-democracies so that the threat of violence on a national and a global level would be turned into a means for liberal-democracies to reinvent themselves and to achieve a higher degree of inclusive democracy than that they have so far presented.

This may sound somewhat visionary, but the hope is that from the challenge of movements using violence as a threat against the citizens of democracy there might emerge a new type of democracy capable of meeting that threat by undermining the validity of the claim that it is only through violence that group demands can be satisfied.

8 Democracy in Times of Risk and Uncertainty

The purpose of this concluding chapter is to explore the wider implications of the preceding analysis for understanding democracy and its prospects in the present situation of world politics, with a particular focus on the question of political violence. The earlier chapters explored the relationship between, on the one hand, democracy as an ideal excluding violence, and on the other hand the political reality in which violence is ever-present, challenging the theoretical incompatibility of democratic politics and violent political action. We have seen how violence has been used both by movements opposing the ideal of democracy as well as by groups seeking inclusion in a democratic community who use violence as a means to draw attention to the reality of their exclusion and marginalisation. We have also seen how democratic states use violence in self-defence, but equally how state violence is often practised beyond such limits, for example in policies and actions which claim to spread democracy on a world-wide basis. Likewise, we have seen how semi-democratic regimes have used violence to contain and repress oppositional challenges to state power, and the ways in which this can lead to the normalisation and privatisation of political violence. In extreme cases, at least for a limited period of time, as we saw with the Kenyan example, this can lead to the undermining of the state's monopoly of violence. In such a situation something approaching a Hobbesian state of nature or 'war of all against all' is present, in which gangs exercise power, not in the sense of Hannah Arendt's definition of power as consensual and legitimate, but in a crude sense of 'might is right'.

The Kenyan example pointed to the need not just for the state to hold a monopoly of the means of violence to guarantee the rights of democratic participation, but also for institutional reform. Such institutional reform, if successful, would create checks and controls on state power and equally importantly would provide mediating institutions to validate elections so that citizens would not feel the need to 'take to the streets' in order to express their political will.

The obvious implication of all of the examples given in previous chapters is that violence is present everywhere in political life, in democracies as well as in societies seeking, successfully or not, to make a transition to democratic rule. It also seems to be the case, as demonstrated in Chapter 6 above, that the apparently irresistible sweep of globalisation has intensified rather than diminished the likelihood of political violence. This is the case not merely because of the attempts to spread democracy (of a certain kind) on a world-wide basis and to practise the politics of 'humanitarian intervention'. It is also the case because movements of population and the power of global economic flows make the nation-state less able to contain outbreaks of violence and less powerful in establishing a community of citizens who renounce violence as a political weapon in favour of reciprocal dialogue and discussion between equals. Furthermore, in the real world of politics, democratic states employ the threat of violence and carry out that threat in order to defend their existence. Political violence is used both by states and by non-state movements, and indeed the sphere of the political is inherently bound up with the use of means of violence. It was for that reason that Max Weber insisted that those who engage in political action are dealing with 'demonic' forces whose impact can be devastating if they are not controlled (Weber 1970 [1919]). If the sphere of the political is inseparable from violence, then how can violence be excluded from politics, and how could the promise held out in our first chapter, the substitution of democratic procedures for those of political violence, be fulfilled?

This concluding chapter seeks to summarise the nature and

degree of the challenge which violence presents to democratic politics, and to review the causes and reasons for the use of violence. In the light of the seemingly inevitable and ubiquitous presence of violence and its use as a political weapon by both states and non-state movements, what are the implications of violence for democratic politics in supposedly established as well as in would-be democratic political systems? Does violence make it impossible to create and maintain democracy? Is violence a permanent presence which risks eroding the checks on the democratic state and which also represents a serious obstacle to the establishment of democratic processes where these do not as yet exist?

The answer to be given here is organised around the three headings of *the degree and nature* of the challenge of political violence, the *reasons for its persistence*, and the *ways in which the recourse to violence can be reduced* by both state and non-state actors. The argument proceeds on the assumption that the ideal of excluding violence altogether from democratic politics can never be fully realised, but that there can be responses of the democratic state to the challenge of violence which minimise that threat and which are in accordance with democratic norms. By the same token, violence poses a constant impediment to the transition to democracy and to the solid implantation of democratic forms of politics. This is especially true (the Kenyan case is again highly relevant here) if violence is diffused throughout society and comes to be accepted as a normal way of doing politics. This evidently blocks the path to the acceptance of democratic dialogue and to the installation of a community of equal citizens who accept each other as entitled to mutual respect and to the enjoyment of rights of participation in political life. Yet here too the task of applied political theory is to suggest ways in which the threat of violence can be minimised, even if it can never be totally eradicated, and to propose a normative response to violence involving both institutional reform and a transformed discourse of politics.

How Serious is the Challenge of Violence?

Starting then with an assessment of the degree and nature of the threat of violence to democracy in established and yet-to-be established forms, the challenge is evidently less serious in the former than in the latter. In the former, there are movements of Islamic fundamentalism like Al Qaeda which threaten violent attacks on the citizens of Western democratic societies. Equally significant, as has been demonstrated throughout the text, the procedures of democratic politics are jeopardised when nationalist groups use violence to draw attention to the failure of the state to recognise distinct cultural and national identities. Moreover, economic and social inequalities provide the basis for explosions of violence when the contrast is great between the aspirations of citizen equality and the realities of social deprivation and political exclusion, as witnessed by the urban riots in France in 2005, to cite only one example. Nevertheless, in these situations (of established democratic polities), violence, while constantly threatening as a problem, arises within the framework of democratic politics. This means that it does not risk undermining the democratic fabric of the society as a whole or endanger the processes of democratic discussion in general.

By contrast, the challenge of violence is more threatening in societies where the democratic state is weak, or indeed where state power is unable to impose itself over the territory it supposedly controls. In such a situation the attempt to substitute democratic norms in the place of physical force is far more difficult, all the more so where ethnic differences and the social tensions which they cause make for very weak bonds of solidarity between citizens. The most deadly examples of political violence occur then where the state is weak, and where those holding state power seek to prop up the state by calling in the aid of private groups of armed persons whose power comes from their use of violence. In such cases violence pervades the whole of society and the state loses its legitimacy, becoming as violent and as partial as those groups practising violence in the wider society. Some of them are sponsored by the state, as was clear in the case of Kenya. There are thus no state restraints on inter-communal violence, and whatever security is available to citizens can only be purchased through the protection of gangs which themselves use violence.

The answer to the first question, then, concerning the degree and nature of the challenge of violence to democracy in contemporary politics, has to be that violence exists as a permanent or ongoing challenge to democratic politics both in established democracies and in would-be democracies, but that it is a more radical threat in the latter than in the former. It is also important to recognise different dimensions of the challenge of violence, both national and international. On the national level, violence erupts when groups feel that the political system at that level does not allow the participation and equality proclaimed in theory by democratic norms. We also, however, have to recognise that violence has international dimensions and that globalisation has caused the challenge of violence to take new forms. Indeed, here lies the novelty of contemporary violence and the forms it takes compared with earlier periods. Violence is inseparable from politics itself, and the aspiration of democratic politics must be to minimise the recourse to violence as a political weapon. Yet the new forms that violence takes in the modern world stem largely from globalisation and its consequences. In the first place this is true because of the networked form of social movements which are not limited to a national context but linked in international forms and forums as well. Thus movements in a national context, for example those of radical right parties, establish links with similar movements in other nations. However, globalisation and violence are connected in deeper ways. The economic instability and shocks which are inseparable from globalisation have a number of consequences which encourage the politics of violence. The movements across borders stimulated by globalisation result in frictions between different cultural groups, whose possible antagonisms are less easily handled by the nation-state, which is itself much weakened in terms of its capacity to mould citizens into a community of democratic solidarity.

While violence is a permanent challenge to the prospects for democratic processes, it is less so in those societies where democratic institutions are more solidly implanted than in would-be democracies. However, if that suggests some grounds for optimism, at least for the citizens of established democracies, such optimism, if it is to be valid, has to be tempered in various ways. Two are particularly relevant here: the first is to recognise that, for reasons discussed in detail above, globalisation leads to new forms of violence and arouses new motivations for violence. The second is to acknowledge that the new global scope of politics encourages attempts to spread democracy world-wide and thus arouses local movements of resistance and opposition, some of them employing nationalist rhetoric and the language of anti-imperialism. We thus arrive at a twofold conclusion: first that violence remains a serious challenge to democracy, even in established democracies; second that some of the forms it has taken in contemporary politics are more intractable than others, and that this is so because of the ways in which globalisation has stimulated the use of violence. Globalisation creates new sources of insecurity at the same time as it provides certain opportunities for communication, mutual reinforcement, encouragement and demonstration to movements intent on using violence as a political tool.

Therefore in some respects violence remains a more intractable problem for contemporary politics, despite the spread of democratic aspirations world-wide. Indeed, the paradox is that attempts at liberalisation and democratisation, even if not imposed 'from outside' by dominant powers, may exacerbate violence, or stimulate the recourse to violence. The example of Kenya is relevant here, yet again. The movement there away from *de jure* one-party politics to multi-party politics can be seen in an optimistic light, as witnessed by the 2007 presidential and parliamentary elections where contests were open and closely fought. Yet violence is more likely if power is open to some degree of popular choice, especially where the stakes are very high, since state power confers substantial benefits on those who exercise it in terms of economic gain and political patronage. This is because the high stakes lead the holders of state power to use and to encourage violence in their desperate attempt to retain that power. Such state-sponsoring of private violence leads to a dangerous situation of the normalisation of violence, both on the part of the state and equally on the part of those seeking to take over state power for themselves. Democracy or movements towards democracy in such cases lead not to the diminution of violence but to its proliferation and extension. The paradox here is that democracy does not exclude violence but stimulates it, in the absence of a strong or at least effective state with at least enough legitimacy to be able to secure democratic processes and discourage citizens from taking to the streets.

It is for this reason that the whole debate about 'sequencing' is an important one in the literature on democratisation, with some scholars insisting that in the absence of an effective state with its mechanisms of control over the territory attempts at democratisation and liberalisation will lead to further outbreaks of violence. The implication then is that before moves towards democratisation can take place, a process of state-building has to be embarked on. State-building is a prerequisite for democratisation, or for democratisation in the absence of corrosive violence. In Chapter 3 reference was made to the analysis offered by Branch and Cheeseman, focusing on the prerequisites of democratisation and liberalisation as involving 'basic state capacity, the effective rule of law, and an agreed national identity'. Without securing those three desiderata, 'the reintroduction of multi-partyism may exacerbate underlying tensions which the state is powerless to manage' (Branch and Cheeseman 2008: 26). This suggests that in order to prevent violence (or at least to diminish its impact) in the context of democratising or liberalising systems, the path must go through institutional reform. This reform must aim at the creation of an effective state able to preserve its monopoly of violence in order to prevent the privatisation of violence and its diffusion throughout society, as was evident in the aftermath of the Kenyan elections of December 2007.

However, the project of institutional reform must involve more elements than this. It should be made clear here that we are talking of means to mitigate the challenge of violence in the context of democratising or liberalising societies. A different agenda presents itself in the context of established democratic societies. In the former context, it is not just a question of establishing an effective state which is able to secure its monopoly over the means of violence. What is also required are institutions which secure the trust of enough of its citizens, if not all of them, that they are not tempted or encouraged to take to the streets or to resort to direct physical confrontation as a way of expressing grievances or making political demands. In the absence of an effective rule of law and of institutions seen as fair and able to mediate on matters such as disputed election results, the chances of containing violence are severely limited. The political institutions are seen as creatures of the government, as was the case with the Kenyan election commission, whose independence had been severely compromised by the Kibaki government so that they were not trusted as a means of judging whether or not the electoral process had been interfered with.

The nature of the challenge of violence is thus that it impedes the establishment of democracy in societies seeking to move towards democracy. In established democratic societies the risk is that of extending the power of the security organs of the state, and thereby undermining the mutual trust between citizens in the attempt to fulfil the necessary task of opposing genuine threats to their security. Thus violence tends to destabilise democracy, whether in the case of established democracies or what are here called 'democracies in the making'. This concluding chapter seeks to develop arguments which point to ways in which the destabilising threat of violence can be averted. How should democratic states respond to the challenge of violence, and how can would-be democracies prevent violence and its diffusion throughout society from impeding the installation of democratic values and procedures?

How Should Democracies Respond to Violence?

Faced with movements of violence, states in general have a variety of possible responses, ranging from negotiation to repression. Appropriate responses depend on the particular form the violence takes, and on the reasons which motivate individuals and groups to resort to violence. With those who are fundamentally unwilling to accept democratic procedures, and who see a democratic system as evil and illegitimate, there can be no peaceful negotiation or compromise. However, if the arguments deployed in earlier chapters of this book are valid, this form or source of violence is the preserve of only a minority of those using violence for political ends. Violence arises when people feel threatened or feel that their identity and culture are either not recognised, or in extreme cases are under direct attack. Under this general heading of lack of respect and lack of recognition come violent movements of a nationalist kind, where there is a 'mismatch' between state and nation, in the sense that national identity is not reflected or taken into account in the state of which the particular nation is part. Lack of recognition and denial of identity here constitute crucial causes of political violence. These are increasingly relevant in the present political situation and replace the 'traditional' causes of political violence which were more significant in the past.

This contrast between 'old' and 'new' forms of violence needs further explanation. By 'old' forms of violence are to be understood movements which used violence to oppose or overthrow democracy and replace it with an authoritarian system, whether of fascist or more traditional dictatorial form. Violence historically was also a political weapon used by subordinate classes to establish their entry into the political system and to capture democratic rights denied them by ruling groups. Violence was thus the preserve of broad movements with a class basis seeking either to overthrow or prevent democratic regimes, or else to secure democratic rights of participation. New forms of violence have some points of contact with these older historical forms: political violence is still practised by groups who wish to secure entry into the democratic system and who seek a greater degree of inclusion in it. However the agents of political violence are more likely to be groups whose identity is marked by cultural points of reference, and who seek political inclusion with the main aim of gaining recognition for that distinct culture. They seek to carve out a space within democratic society as a means of securing recognition of a particular identity, more in the sense of gaining an enclave within the broader shelter of democratic society and exercising political rights in defence of that particular cultural identity. Rather than claiming democratic rights as a means for participation and broader civic engagement, the tendency is to invoke those rights for the purposes of protection of one particular identity.

Hence the sources of violence in the contemporary world in the context of established democratic societies have to be differentiated from those of the past. The agents of violence today are different from the broad class-based movements of earlier times which sought entry into the democratic system or tried to overthrow it entirely. The new causes of violence stem from perceptions of injustice and lack of recognition, from demands for inclusion on the part of groups who claim that they are denied full citizen status and proper social equality, and from claims for recognition of distinct national identities.

The important question in practical terms is the nature of the policies and attitudes which could meet this challenge of violence both within national boundaries and internationally. How should states respond to the challenge of violence in ways which are consistent with democratic norms? What modes of democratic arrangement might limit the different threats of violence faced by democratic and would-be democratic societies? What must be avoided are responses which exacerbate the danger or the challenge. If democracies respond by treating all violent challenges as a security problem, the risk is a twofold one. In the first place responses of a 'securitisation' kind are liable to deepen the problem by eroding the democratic rights and liberties which are foundational of or fundamental to the liberal-democratic order. Furthermore they also tend to reinforce the powers of the security organs of the state thus inviting a form of 'slippage' to an executive-dominated state in which the democratic and scrutinising agents of the state apparatus are marginalised relative to the agents of security. In this case, liberal-democracies move towards what could be called a 'security state' rather than the 'market state' analysed by Bobbitt. In turn this erodes the trust and mutual confidence of citizens in a democracy and reduces further the chances of democratic community, analysed in Chapter 1 as a vital prerequisite for an inclusive political association. Finally, repressive state action, and the presentation of the problem as being one of 'security' alone, are both liable to give disaffected minority groups more justification for their violent actions, since they feel they are being victimised and further excluded from the effective exercise of citizenship rights.

The response of democratic societies thus has to be a more nuanced and broader one than that of 'securitisation', even if the latter has to be practised in answer to violent movements who do not accept the legitimacy of democratic politics. Different forms of violence require different reactions. The violence of those who oppose democracy in principle and who commit themselves to international movements in radical opposition to democratic regimes will only be effective if their ranks are swollen beyond their 'hard core' of irreconcilable fanatics. The reinforcement of such groups comes from others who feel that liberal-democracies are systematically prejudiced against them in various ways, so that violence of an unremitting kind is the only way in which inclusion in the full citizen body can be gained. The core of the analysis given here stems from the belief that alternative responses must be found beyond those of repression and securitisation, so that those who are in irreconcilable hostility to liberal-democracy will remain a small minority whose threat is dealt with by normal policing measures appropriate for the security services and the democratically controlled agencies of the state.

The broader argument developed here is that in established democracies a different form of democracy has to be envisaged which changes the nature of democracy so that those who might be tempted towards the use of violence become convinced that it does not offer a viable means of securing recognition or of pursuing their political interests. Only by such radical transformation of democratic institutions and the discourse of politics can the prospects for democracy in an age of risk and uncertainty be enhanced and a degree of democratic security achieved. The implications for developing democracies are equally oriented to the goal of institutional creation, rather than transformation, in the sense that the need is for institutions that can persuade people to place their trust in them rather than have recourse to violent physical confrontation, even if that may be the only form of political action available before the creation of such institutions able to mediate conflict.

Institutional Reform and Reform of Discourse

The argument proposed here is that institutional reform is to be complemented by a new language of politics. What such a new political discourse would involve would be a strengthened conception of citizenship in which ideas of shared debate and common interest would replace the heightened individualism which is characteristic of contemporary political discourse. Only when people see each other in a stronger sense as citizens in a shared political enterprise could there be a chance of rejecting violence as a political weapon.

What is involved here is what Neal Ascherson once described as a situation of 'forum politics' in which previously antagonistic political actors are forced or force themselves to engage in dialogue with each other and are thus provided with opportunities to hear the views of those with whom dialogue was previously impossible (Ascherson 1992: 223). The problem with contemporary liberal-democratic systems is that they are lacking in institutions which would facilitate such dialogue between and among distinct groups of citizens. There have been some interesting discussions of this issue in recent analyses dealing with the UK government's attempts to get British Muslims 'on side' or to wean them away from temptations to resort to violence, or to support those who do (Briggs 2010; Pantucci 2010). The UK government policy in this respect, according to Pantucci, risks alienation rather than gaining support from sections of the Muslim community. Within the context of national political communities this seems to suggest the need to create new institutions which would enable democratic dialogue of two kinds. The first would be between agents of the state, such as the police, and sections of the community, in an ongoing dialogue. The second would be institutions capable of facilitating dialogue between civil society groups thereby preventing the encapsulation of society into different groups with weak relationships or none at all. In this respect then, the new language or discourse of politics called for here could not be something artificially imposed from above, but would be fostered through the working of institutions which demand dialogue between citizens themselves. The perspective here is derived from republican or neo-republican principles, according to which a process of institutional reform helps to transform the attitudes of those who are called on to work in such institutions and stimulates the development of their capacities.

However, we have to return to the distinction between established democracies and those societies in which democracy is not solidly implanted. In established democratic societies, violence is certainly not absent: it has erupted in such events as 9/11, the explosions in Madrid and London, and in nationalist conflicts such as those in the Basque country and in Northern Ireland. In societies like Mexico it is criminal violence which challenges and erodes the state's monopoly of the use of violence. However serious all these instances of violence were, with the possible exception of Mexico (in certain parts of the country), they have not made it impossible for citizens to pursue their daily lives in conditions of peace and security. In a wider global context, by contrast, war and inter-communal conflict lead to violence on such a scale that 'normal' life is barely possible. We thus have to understand violence on an ascending scale, from particular riots and violent acts of protest to violence as practised by powerful states intent on regime-change. The obvious examples here are Afghanistan and Iraq, but beyond that there are others, where massive state power has been deployed in the cause of so-called humanitarian intervention, as in Kosovo and Bosnia-Herzegovina. In these latter cases violent intervention was employed in an attempt to stop the use of violence by the states of those particular areas which saw themselves as the agent of a particular ethnic group. Nationalism and ethnic conflict have thus fuelled violence in extreme ways. These examples of so-called 'new wars', occasioned in many instances by nationalist and ethnic conflict, are the prime cases of violence in contemporary politics.

Can violence of this kind be tamed, and are violent forms of humanitarian intervention adequate means to do this? We have to consider the impact of such violence in the broader global context. In the same way as violence can become 'normalised' in a national context, such as in Kenya where it was considered an acceptable way of regulating political disputes, so too can violence come to be seen as a regular instrument of international politics, carried out by states who practise so-called humanitarian intervention with the purpose of creating a world order favourable to democracy.

The main violent challenges to democracy on a global level come from groups and movements which fundamentally reject the value and validity of democracy, and on the other hand from those who wish to turn the state into a vehicle for imposing one ethnic, cultural or national identity on all those living in the same territory, as was exemplified in cases like those of Kosovo and Bosnia-Herzegovina. Yet these are not the only sources of political violence, which can erupt in situations where there are no agreed procedures or institutions through which the mediation of conflict is possible. Where there is no shared culture of citizenship, people do not regard each other as mutually entitled to share in the process of political deliberation and debate. The causes of political violence can therefore be traced to feelings of insecurity, lack of respect, and the absence of stable institutions which permit a joint process of democratic exchange of views. In the absence of an effective state, no such institutions of deliberation are possible and civil and political order can easily break down. We thus need to differentiate between the established democracies where there are such institutions, if only in imperfect form, and authoritarian systems or 'democracies in the making' where violence practised by the state becomes an accepted means of enforcing order.

The study by Geoffrey Robinson of the violence practised in 1999 by the Indonesian military and paramilitary groups against the East Timor separatist movement shows well that violence is not the inevitable result of ethnic difference, diverse religious identities, or of socio-economic inequalities. His study of East Timor bears out some of the implications which were drawn from the earlier discussion of the violence in Kenya in 2007. In both cases violence developed as a result of a conscious decision of those holding state power to use physical force to maintain that power and to repress forcibly those who seemed to present a threat. In Robinson's words, mass violence 'required a substantial measure of conscious organisation and a strategic decision by state authorities to deploy violence to achieve a political objective' (Robinson 2010: 230). In 1999 the Indonesian army forcibly enlisted people into pro-Indonesian militias in East Timor. In many cases this was a forced mobilisation. The power of the Indonesian army was thus used to spread violence through the agency of these militia organisations, with the advantage for the Indonesian authorities that they could deny their own responsibility for the violence by claiming that it was the work of civil society organisations, in other words of the people of East Timor themselves. Robinson's analysis brings out two points which are central to the present discussion of how violence by state and non-state actors could be minimised. In the first instance, the East Timor case has shown that, rather than being the result of a spontaneous outburst of ethnic hatred, the violence was intentionally deployed for political ends by the Indonesian armed forces. This involved the deployment of militias which had been forcibly recruited, so that, just as in the case of Kenya, violence was diffused through the whole of society and spread by the actions of those holding state power.

Furthermore the use of this state-sponsored violence was encouraged by a pre-existing culture of terror and its acceptance within the Indonesian army as a normal and justifiable mode of action. In turn this had deeper historical roots, as Robinson explains: the colonial powers had themselves often employed local militias to fight on their behalf. Thus the normalisation or acceptance of violence and physical force had long been part of the mindset of Indonesia, going back to colonial times and even earlier. The conclusion reached by Robinson's study thus has wider implications. Political violence is in many cases not some natural or spontaneous outburst, but is the result of intentional action on the part of those who hold state power. In the cases of Indonesia and Kenya, the holders of state power sponsored and encouraged the use of violence by groups outside the state. They diffused violence in the form of paramilitary gangs and militias throughout the wider society. This process contributed to a situation in which extreme violence in the form of rape, killing and destruction of property was seen as legitimate or acceptable means of achieving a political goal. In the Indonesian/East Timor case the aim was to prevent the secession of East Timor and the means used involved the violent intimidation of those struggling for that secession. The conclusion is therefore that political violence is not an inevitable result of difference, whether that be ethnic, religious, cultural or class-based, but that political violence becomes a serious challenge to democracy when it is consciously practised as a political weapon, whether by holders of state power or by non-state movements.

A similar conclusion is reached by an authority on the situation in Chechnya. John Dunlop writes of the (second) war in Chechnya that it 'broke out because of a conviction on the part of a significant segment of the Russian leadership that ethnic grievances can be resolved through the use of force and through "black" operations rather than through patient negotiations' (Dunlop 1998: 223). Clearly, such examples – Kenya, Indonesia, Russia/Chechnya – are cases of state and state-sponsored violence. They suggest that a particular culture of violence can be established in which political action is carried on through means of violent repression. This in turn sparks off movements themselves prepared to use violence against the state, preferring force to 'patient negotiations', so that force seems to be the only means through which political demands can be made. In the same way, writers on the struggle of the Kurds talk about a 'deep state' within Turkey. This 'deep state' used illegal methods to suppress opposition and to decapitate the leadership of oppositional movements (Gunter 2008). We are thus returned to the question of how such violence might be averted and how, in unpropitious circumstances, institutions could be created which make holders of state power and those opposing them reject violence as a means of political action.

Optimistic versus Pessimistic Scenarios

This concluding discussion will oscillate between two contrasting perspectives, which can be simplistically labelled the pessimistic scenario and the optimistic scenario, with the final balance falling in favour of the optimistic. On the pessimistic side of the equation there is the global spread of violence, the greater ability of both states and those opposing them to inflict damage and harm on civilians, and the relative weakness of those institutions, notably the nation-state, which have in the past functioned effectively to limit violence. New forms of violence have arisen in the global arena employing new weapons and advanced technologies: 'Violence, both embodied and structural, is carried through the new possibilities for the extension of power across time and space, not only reshaping the kinds of violence that occur within localised struggles but making new patterns of violence possible' (Grenfell and James 2009: 7). Political violence therefore occurs in wider arenas and with more devastating effects. Globalisation has intensified violence in a number of ways. Through the displacement and migration of millions of people it has given rise to new conflicts and sources of tension, created wider zones of conflict, and enabled the domination of one super-power with a long reach. Democracy, paradoxically, has become the justification for violent intervention which uses as its pretext the spreading of the benefits of democracy world-wide. In that sense violence is no longer localised but is carried out by movements, both state and anti-state, which have a global and international scope.

This breakdown in the means of controlling violence and steering it into the arena of peaceful compromise and reconciliation, is not, however, the full picture. We have seen above that a culture of violence can be spread by the conscious decision of holders of state power to unleash political violence and to sponsor groups using it. There are nevertheless still means of controlling violence, located in three spheres of activity in which opposition to a culture of violence and its normalisation as a means of political activity might be developed. The three spheres of activity are those of states and governments, of civil society organisations, and finally of citizens as political actors. If governments themselves unleash violence through a conscious decision, then equally this means that they have the ability to consciously reject the use of violence to maintain their power. As we saw in the Kenya case, the decision to use violence is more likely when the stakes are high. In a 'zero-sum' situation when state power is the key to wealth and control of assets there will be a much greater determination to hang on to such power. The corollary is that any means, including those of violence, are seen as justifiable in order to maintain possession of state power.

How then can the culture of violence and the temptation to resort to it be transformed with reference to states and governments, the first of our three elements? If state power is made less of an 'all or nothing' institution, then its attractions will be diminished and the overriding temptation to hold on to it at all costs will be less. This entails there being some decentralisation and diffusion of power so that the situation is not as it was in the Kenyan case, when the strengthening of the executive power of the president meant that power brought with it massive rewards in terms of wealth, so that the alternative to holding on to the state became unthinkable for those who had enjoyed its benefits. If a political order is established which is not a 'winner takes all' type of system, then the stakes of power-holding become lowered so that the system is not one of 'all or nothing' in which those who hold state power are rewarded with dominance over society, while those who have lost out in the struggle for power face marginalisation and in some cases extinction.

The second requirement for mitigating the threat of violence is the creation of institutions which can control the holders of executive power in order to erect obstacles to their use and sponsorship of violence. In the cases cited already of Indonesia and Kenya, elements of the state apparatus 'farmed out' violence to private gangs and (in the case of Indonesia) forcibly recruited militia. They were able to do this because of their freedom and autonomy of action. An effective judiciary and institutions capable of applying the rule of law would have been able to curb such recourse to violence by denying those who held state power access to the financial resources needed to sponsor violent action by social groups. Liberalisation and democratisation can provoke the use of violence unless there are institutions present which restrain holders of state power from actions that encourage the spread of violence as a political weapon. Such institutions would therefore contribute to making violence and its use in politics unacceptable, and in that way install a culture of what Dunlop calls 'patient negotiation' rather than the use of force to settle differences (Dunlop 1998: 223).

If governments are prevented from using violence as a means of staying in power, then this prevents the poisonous spread of violence throughout the wider society. Of course this is easier said than done, because as the Kenya case shows, in the absence of any effective and neutral institutions for controlling the executive power its holders will not be restrained from violent methods. In turn this stimulates an equal and opposite reaction from the citizens of that society. With regard to civil society organisations, they too have to be seen as a means of preventing the recourse to violence and of instilling a culture of democratic negotiation rather than physical force. In the light of what has just been said about the role of the holders of state power in sponsoring violence in order to hold on to power, it needs to be made clear that the problem of violence and democracy is a broader one. While governments are indeed agents of violence, it is only when their attempts to stir up violence in the broader society meet with an equally violent response that this becomes a serious challenge to a democratic society. Our concluding reflections must therefore be on the causes of the acceptance and pervasive nature of violence in instances of inter-communal violence, terrorist activity and riots, all of which involve the use of physical force to attain political ends. It should be understood here that what is in question is not the kind of revolutionary violence exercised by mass movements and revolutionary parties seeking to take over the state, as in Russia in 1917. It is rather a range of actions, from street riots and violent protests, to orchestrated terrorist actions as exemplified by 9/11, to outbreaks of inter-communal violence such as occurred in Kenya or India. To these could be added examples of violence perpetrated by nationalist groups like ETA and IRA. The theme here is not violence carried out by the state, but violent actions carried out by members of 'civil society', whether for purposes of protest at exclusion or in pursuit of nationalist aims of autonomy or self-rule in an independent nation-state.

The eruption of violence and the substitution of physical force as a means of expressing political demands have to be understood as a symptom of the breakdown or weakness of democratic community. In a democratic community, in an ideal sense, its members may regard each other as opponents holding different views about how society should be organised, but they are seen at the same time as participants in some common or shared association of democratic politics. This may not preclude bitter disputes and conflicts over values and over the ends the democratic association should pursue, but such conflicts take place within a framework of mutual recognition between antagonists who recognise each other as equally entitled to participate in a process of debate and political contest. Violence erupts when one section of the population is denied the status of an equally entitled participant in political struggle. A democratic society does indeed need conflict since conflict and opposition are inevitable in any complex society. However, democratic politics requires institutions to mediate such antagonisms since where these institutions are lacking conflict will turn into violent physical confrontation.

One of the main paradoxes of democracy is that in certain of its forms it can itself stimulate and produce violence, especially if democracy is conceived in a simple 'majoritarian' form as the will of the majority. If that majority denies to the minority either cultural recognition or effective participation in making and influencing the law, then there is no reason for that minority to reject violence and accept involvement in political institutions if those institutions are seen as nothing more than structures for enforcing majority rule. Yet in the 'culture of contentment' analysed by John Kenneth Galbraith those who are in a position of (relative) affluence are unwilling to pay taxes to support or assist those economically and socially deprived (Galbraith 1992). If the latter are denied a 'voice' in the political process, or at least a genuinely effective means of expression, then violence in the form of urban riots and destruction of property is a likely response to this exclusion from genuine civic involvement. If violence threatens democracy as a result of exclusion and failure of recognition, how can these defects be remedied so that violence is not seen as a means of political action? The answer, so we have argued, has to follow Habermas' suggestion of the need for some kind of '*Schliessung*' or 'closure', which will fulfil the same function for the contemporary age as the nation-state did for an earlier period of modernity. By such a '*Schliessung*' is to be understood a political community which in some way answers the needs of those who are subject to it. The nation-state used to be effective in providing institutions which integrated the members of the citizen body and subjected them to a common process of education (socialisation in the broadest sense). The result was that they saw each other as fellow-citizens with whom dialogue, if not agreement, was possible. Democratic community achieved through the nation-state ruled out violence, or at least minimised it between fellow-citizens, though it did not rule out imperialist violence practised against the populations of what became colonies of Western nation-states. Nor did the democratic community of the nation-state preclude racism and the marginalisation of ethnic minorities and immigrants who had to 'prove' themselves worthy of integration into the ranks of 'true members' of the nation-state. Given this, one should not exaggerate or mythologize the degree of citizenship as it was attained by the nation-state.

However, with these limits duly acknowledged, it can be said that the nation-state was an effective political and social institution which, through its establishment of democratic community, reduced the risk of violence between fellow-citizens. It not only provided institutions for mediating conflict, but enforced a common education system which gave its citizens a common history in the sense of a shared narrative, explaining how they came to share in that common legacy. We are here evoking Renan's famous analysis of the nation as a 'grand solidarity', a daily plebiscite of those who wished to continue living together (Renan 1992 [1882]: 54). Those who write the final obituary of the nation-state may be premature in their analysis. However, it is undeniable that the nation-state is today less able to perform its functions of reducing or containing violence, for several reasons. Given the multicultural character of the citizen body, it is now more difficult, perhaps impossible, to create a feeling of solidarity through a shared narrative of, say, British history or French history, or whatever nation is in question.

Moreover in many cases the nation-state is the problem rather than the solution, especially where it functions as an apparatus to maintain the domination not (as in the Marxist conception) of a ruling class but of a specific ethnic and cultural group, which results in the exclusion or victimisation of those of different cultural affiliation. In such cases the state does not provide institutions for mediating conflict, but represses members of other groups through violence, thereby provoking counter-violence in its turn. Political violence is an ever-present possibility both in established democracies and in societies seeking to establish democracy on firmer foundations. It can never be totally eradicated because it is a permanent weapon deployed by those who are excluded from the mainstream institutions of the society and who see violence as the only possible means of redressing that situation. Furthermore violence is enhanced by the insecurities arising out of globalisation and the fears that process provokes. This is especially true in light of the greater cultural heterogeneity of modern societies and the danger that particular groups of an ethnic or cultural kind see the state as 'their' state, which involves the marginalisation of others of different cultural affiliation.

It would be wrong to exaggerate the degree of violence involved and conclude that this makes democracy impossible. However the present situation is one of extreme paradox, in the sense that throughout the world democracy is held up to be the universal desirable model, yet this very allegiance to the ideals of democracy brings with it a greater degree of violence. Since democracy is claimed to be the only way in which a safer and more secure world can be attained, it is 'exported' and imposed, in one particular model, by dominant states and powers, such as the United States (aided by Britain and other states). In turn this leaves democracy open to counter-attack, often (as in Iraq and Afghanistan) by violent forces who claim that the democracy supposedly being brought to them is but a mask for Western domination and the imperialist acquisition of economic resources. In this way the attempts to spread democracy, often by means of violence, in turn spark off a violent response. Similarly, while democracy is given near-universal approval and all groups demand participation in political life, this desirable goal is made more difficult as a result of the insecurities arising out of globalisation. They make it more problematic to create an inclusive state, since particular groups hold on to state power as a means of defending themselves against the challenges of excluded groups who also want access to that power. Democracy thus turns against itself and violent conflicts are the result.

The conclusion thus has to be that violence is inseparable from the workings and nature of democratic politics, but that such politics involve a constant and ongoing attempt to ward off the threat of violence. In present conditions, this attempt very often takes the form of a 'security' type of response that enhances the role of the state as a policeman which through its security agencies is able to repress violent challenges. Yet it is doubtful whether that kind of security response can succeed in establishing the democratic community which alone could provide a more hopeful answer to the problem of political violence.

That community has to be built on a supra-national or global scale, since only on that level could it introduce the 'closure' necessary to control those powerful economic forces that presently escape democratic scrutiny. In practical terms, in order to provide the economic and social resources for a genuine democratic community in which all can achieve the status of equal interlocutors, there has to be more influence over those economic forces which have undermined the nation-state and reduced its ability to limit violence. New institutions have to be created or developed, on an international scale, which will fulfil the same function that the nation-state did.

We can thus conclude on a hopeful rather than a pessimistic note. Violence, whether exercised by states or non-state movements, is indeed a challenge to democracy since it undermines the procedures of rational discourse involving all participants seeking to convince each other rather than to impose their will by means of force. While violence can never be eradicated, since it is a permanent weapon held in reserve by those who are excluded and marginalised, it can be managed through the creation of democratic community. If violence arises in part as a reaction on the part of those who are excluded from the democratic community, the extension of democratic forms of association in a more inclusive way would reduce the incentive to use violence. It would now appeal only to those who valued violence for its own sake rather than as a rational tool to attain political ends.

This book has thus reached its end point. It began by explaining that democracy needs both community and conflict and that its aim is to avoid violent conflict by providing means of mediating disputes through genuine debate. However, as we saw in subsequent chapters, violence is used both by the democratic state and by those challenging it for various reasons – whether to overthrow democracy or to seek inclusion in it. In many cases, actions carried out by contemporary liberal-democratic states have only deepened the problem, as the issue is approached as being one of security rather than of extending democratic community. In the case of would-be democracies, the problem is often one of the state and its associated institutions not having any credibility in terms of their capacity to respond to various grievances in a neutral way. The solution is therefore one which involves a global or international set of institutions. The institutions of such a global commonwealth of citizens would diminish the risk of violence by bringing into its ranks not just states and their representatives, but also a wider range of groups from civil society, including those who practise violence. The latter would then have a forum in which they would have to explain their use of violence and seek responses from those states and political communities from which they are presently excluded. We can thus conclude with reference to two basic ideas: first, the creation of a cosmopolitan set of institutions able to offer the opportunity of democratic participation to a wider range of actors than nation-states are able to at the moment. Second, the development of institutions in which democratic deliberation among that wide range of participants is possible and which thus provide credible alternatives to the politics of violence as a means of resolving conflict. Only in such ways can there be a successful response to the challenge to democracy presented by political violence.

Bibliography

Agamben, Giorgio (2005) *State of Exception*, Chicago: University of Chicago Press.

Anderson, David and Emma Lochery (2008) 'Violence and Exodus in Kenya's Rift Valley: Predictable and Preventable?', *Journal of Eastern African Studies*, Vol. 2, No. 2, pp. 328–43.

Appadurai, Arjun (2006) *Fear of Small Numbers: An Essay on the Geography of Anger*, Durham NC: Duke University Press.

Archibugi, Daniele (2008) *The Global Community of Citizens: Toward Cosmopolitan Democracy*, Princeton NJ: Princeton University Press.

Arendt, Hannah (1973), 'On Violence', in H. Arendt, *Crises of the Republic*, Harmondsworth: Penguin, pp. 83–163.

Ascherson, Neal (1992) '1989 in Eastern Europe', in John Dunn (ed.), *Democracy: The Unfinished Journey, 508BC to AD1993*, Oxford: Oxford University Press.

Aust, Stefan (1987) *The Baader-Meinhof Group: The Inside Story of a Phenomenon*, London: Bodley Head.

Babeuf, François-Noël (1976) *Textes choisis*, edited by Claude Mazauric, Paris: Éditions Sociales.

Balibar, Etienne (2009) 'Violence', *Historical Materialism*, Vol. 17, No. 1, pp. 99–126.

Bauer, Otto (2000) [1924] *The Question of Nationalities and Social Democracy*, edited by E. Nimni, translated by J. O'Donnell, London and Minneapolis: University of Minnesota Press.

Bauman, Zygmunt (2002) *Society Under Siege*, Cambridge: Polity Press.

Beetham, David (2009) 'The Contradictions of Democratization by Force: The Case of Iraq', *Democratization*, Vol. 16, No. 3, pp. 443–55.

Benhabib, Seyla (2002) *The Claims of Culture: Equality and Diversity in the Global Era*, Princeton NJ: Princeton University Press.

Benjamin, Walter (1977) 'Zur Kritik der Gewalt', in W. Benjamin, *Gesammelte Schriften*, edited by Rolf Tiedemann and Hermann Schweppenhäuser, Vol. II, Part 1, Frankfurt: Suhrkamp, pp. 179–203.

Besteman, C. (ed.) (2002) *Violence: A Reader*, Basingstoke: Palgrave Macmillan.

Bigo, Didier and Rob B. J. Walker (2008) 'Le régime de contre-terrorisme global', in D. Bigo, L. Bonelli and T. Deltombe (eds), *Au nom du 11 septembre . . . Les démocraties à l'épreuve de l'antiterrorisme*, Paris: La Découverte.

Bigo, Didier, L. Bonelli and T. Deltombe (eds) (2008) *Au nom du 11 septembre . . . Les démocraties à l'épreuve de l'antiterrorisme*, Paris: La Découverte.

Bobbio, N. (1987) *The Future of Democracy: A Defence of the Rules of the Game*, Cambridge: Polity Press.

Bobbitt, Philip (2008) *Terror and Consent: The Wars for the Twenty-First Century*, London: Allen Lane.

Branch, Daniel and Nic Cheeseman (2008) 'Democratisation, Sequencing, and State Failure in Africa: Lessons from Kenya', *African Affairs*, 108/430, pp. 1–26.

Briggs, Rachel (2010) 'Hearts and Minds and Votes: The Role of Democratic Participation in Countering Terrorism', *Democratization*, Vol. 17, No. 2, pp. 272–85.

Burke, Edmund (1968) [1790] *Reflections on the Revolution in France*, edited by Conor Cruise O'Brien, Harmondsworth: Penguin.

Butler, Judith (2004) *Precarious Life: The Powers of Mourning and Violence*, London: Verso.

Canovan, Margaret (1998) *Nationhood and Political Theory*, Cheltenham: Edward Elgar.

Carothers, Thomas (2002) 'The End of the Transition Paradigm', *Journal of Democracy*, Vol. 13, pp. 5–21.

Carr, Edward H. (1968) *Nationalism and After*, London: Macmillan.

Castells, Manuel (1996) *The Rise of the Network Society*, Oxford: Blackwell.

Chalmers, Damian (2006) 'Political Rights and Political Reason in European Union Law', in W. Sadurski (ed.), *Political Rights under Stress in 21st Century Europe*, Oxford: Oxford University Press, pp. 55–3.

Chase, Malcolm (2007) *Chartism: A New History*, Manchester: Manchester University Press.

Cox, Robert (1993) 'Gramsci, Hegemony and International Relations: An Essay in Method', in S. Gill (ed.), *Gramsci, Historical Materialism, and International Relations*, Cambridge: Cambridge University Press.

de Tocqueville, Alexis (1968) *Democracy in America*, 2 vols, edited by J. P. Mayer and Max Lerner, London: Collins.

Donzelot, Jacques (2006) *Quand la ville se défait: Quelle politique face à la crise des banlieues?*, Paris: Éditions du Seuil.

Dunlop, John B. (1998) *Russia Confronts Chechnya: Roots of a Separatist Conflict*, Cambridge: Cambridge University Press.

Elias, Norbert (1978) *The Civilising Process*, translated by Norman Jephcott, Oxford: Blackwell.

Engels, Friedrich (1973) [1895] 'Introduction to Karl Marx, The Class Struggles in France 1848 to 1850', in Karl Marx and Friedrich Engels, *Selected Works*, Vol. 2, Moscow: Progress Publishers.

English, Richard (2009) *Terrorism: How to Respond*, Oxford: Oxford University Press.

Esping-Andersen, Gosta (1985) *Politics Against Markets: The Social-Democratic Road to Power*, Princeton NJ: Princeton University Press.

Fichte, Johann Gottlieb (1979) *Addresses to the German Nation*, translated by R. F. Jones and G. H. Turnbull, Westport CT: Greenwood Press.

Figes, Orlando (1996) *A People's Tragedy: The Russian Revolution, 1891–1924*, London: Jonathan Cape.

Galbraith, John Kenneth (1992) *The Culture of Contentment*, Boston: Houghton Mifflin.

Gamble, Andrew (1994) *The Free Economy and the Strong State: The Politics of Thatcherism*, Basingstoke: Macmillan.

Geary, Dick (1987) *Karl Kautsky*, Manchester: Manchester University Press.

Gellner, Ernest (1983) *Nations and Nationalism*, Oxford: Blackwell.

Gellner, Ernest (1998) *Nationalism*, London: Phoenix.

Gill, Stephen (ed.) (1993) *Gramsci, Historical Materialism, and International Relations*, Cambridge: Cambridge University Press.

Gilligan, Emma (2010) *Terror in Chechnya: Russia and the Tragedy of Civilians in War*, Princeton NJ: Princeton University Press.

Girardet, Raoul (ed.) (1966) *Le nationalisme français 1871–1914*, Paris: Armand Colin.

Grenfell, Damian and Paul James (2009) 'Debating Insecurity in a Globalising World: An Introduction', in Damian Grenfell and Paul James (eds), *Rethinking Insecurity, War and Violence: Beyond Savage Globalization?* London: Routledge.

Gunter, Michael M. (2008) *The Kurds Ascending: The Evolving Solution to the Kurdish Problem in Iraq and Turkey*, Basingstoke: Palgrave Macmillan.

Gupta, Dipak K. (2008) *Understanding Terrorism and Political Violence: The Life Cycle of Birth, Growth, Transformation and Demise,* London: Routledge.

Habeck, Mary (2006) *Knowing the Enemy: Jihadist Ideology and the War on Terror*, New Haven CT: Yale University Press.

Habermas, Jürgen (1996) 'Citizenship and National Identity', in J. Habermas, *Between Facts and Norms*, Cambridge: Polity Press.

Habermas, Jürgen (2001) *The Postnational Constellation:*

Political Essays, translated, edited and with an introduction by Max Pensky, Cambridge: Polity Press.

Haubrich, Dirk (2006) 'Modern Politics in an Age of Global Terrorism: New Challenges for Domestic Public Policy', *Political Studies*, Vol. 54, No. 2, pp. 399–423.

Hechter, Michael (2000) *Containing Nationalism*, Oxford: Oxford University Press.

Hobbes, Thomas (1968) [1651] *Leviathan*, edited by C. B. Macpherson, Harmondsworth: Penguin.

Hughes, James (2007) *Chechnya: From Nationalism to Jihad*, Philadelphia PA: University of Pennsylvania Press.

Huntington, Samuel P. (1998) *The Clash of Civilisations and the Remaking of World Order*, London: Touchstone Books.

Jabri, Vivienne (2008) 'La torture, une politique de guerre', in Didier Bigo, L. Bonelli and T. Deltombe (eds) (2008) *Au nom du 11 septembre . . . Les démocraties à l'épreuve de l'antiterrorisme*, Paris: La Découverte, pp. 63–75.

James, Paul and Jonathan Friedman (2006) 'Globalizing War: A Critical Introduction', in Paul James and Jonathan Friedman (eds), *Globalization and Violence, Volume 3: Globalizing War and Intervention*, London: Sage.

Keane, J. (1996) *Reflections on Violence*, London: Verso.

Keane, J. (2004) *Violence and Democracy*, Cambridge: Cambridge University Press.

Kymlicka, Will (2001) *Politics in the Vernacular: Nationalism, Multiculturalism and Citizenship*, Oxford: Oxford University Press.

Kymlicka, Will and M. Opalski (eds) (2001) *Can Liberal Pluralism be Exported? Western Political Theory and Ethnic Relations in Eastern Europe*, Oxford: Oxford University Press.

Lawrence, Bruce B. and A. Karim (eds) (2007) *On Violence: A Reader*, Durham NC and London: Duke University Press.

Lazar, Nomi Clair (2009) *States of Emergency in Liberal Democracies*, Cambridge: Cambridge University Press.

Locke, John (1988) [1690] *Two Treatises of Government*, edited by P. Laslett, Cambridge: Cambridge University Press.

Lynch, Gabrielle (2008) 'Courting the Kalenjin: The Failure of Dynasticism and the Strength of the ODM Wave in Kenya's Rift Valley Province', *African Affairs* 107/429, pp. 541–68.

Madison, James, A. Hamilton and J. Jay (1987) [1788] *The Federalist Papers*, edited by Isaac Kramnick, Harmondsworth: Penguin.

Mann, Michael (2005) *The Dark Side of Democracy: Explaining Ethnic Cleansing*, Cambridge: Cambridge University Press.

Markell, Patchen (2000) 'Making Affect Safe for Democracy? On "Constitutional Patriotism"', *Political Theory*, Vol. 28, No. 1, pp. 38–63.

Marx, Karl (1973) [1869] 'The Eighteenth Brumaire of Louis Bonaparte', in Karl Marx, *Surveys from Exile: Political Writings, Vol. 2*, edited by David Fernbach, Harmondsworth: Penguin.

Marx, Karl and Friedrich Engels (1973) [1848] 'Manifesto of the Communist Party', in Karl Marx, *The Revolutions of 1848: Political Writings, Vol. 1*, edited by David Fernbach, Harmondsworth: Penguin.

Mees, Ludger (2003) *Nationalism, Violence and Democracy: The Basque Clash of Identities*, Basingstoke: Palgrave Macmillan.

Menjivar, Cecilia and Néstor Rodríguez (eds) (2005) *When States Kill: Latin America, the U.S., and Technologies of Terror*, Austin TX: University of Texas Press.

Miliband, Ralph (1977) *Marxism and Politics*, Oxford: Oxford University Press.

Muchielli, Laurent and V. Le Goaziou (eds) (2006) *Quand les banlieues brûlent . . . Retour sur les émeutes de novembre 2005*, Paris: La Découverte.

Mueller, Susanne D. (2008) 'The Political Economy of Kenya's Crisis', *Journal of Eastern African Studies*, Vol. 2, No. 2, pp. 185–210.

Nanz, Patrizia (2006) *Europolis: Constitutional Patriotism Beyond the Nation-state*, Manchester: Manchester University Press.

Nef, Jorge and B. Reitner (2009) *The Democratic Challenge:*

Rethinking Democracy and Democratisation, Basingstoke: Palgrave.

Negri, Antonio (1992) *Le pouvoir constituant: Essai sur les alternatives de la modernité*, Paris: Presses Universitaires de France.

Nodia, Ghia (1994) 'Nationalism and Democracy', in L. Diamond and M. F. Plattner (eds), *Nationalism, Ethnic Conflict, and Democracy*, Baltimore and London: Johns Hopkins University Press.

Pantucci, Raffaello (2010) 'A Contest to Democracy? How the UK has Responded to the Current Terrorist Threat', *Democratization*, Vol. 17, No. 2, pp. 251–71.

Parsons, Talcott (1968) *The Structure of Social Action*, New York: The Free Press.

Poulantzas, Nicos (1974) *Fascism and Dictatorship*, London: New Left Books.

Rashid, Ahmed (2008) *Descent into Chaos: How the War Against Islamic Extremism is Being Lost in Pakistan, Afghanistan and Central Asia*, London: Allen Lane.

Renan, Ernest (1992) [1882] 'Qu'est-ce qu'une nation?' in *Qu'est-ce qu'une nation? et autres essais politiques*, edited by Joël Roman, Paris: Presses Pocket.

Renner, Karl (2005), 'State and Nation', in E. Nimni (ed.), *National Cultural Autonomy and its Critics*, London: Routledge.

Riedel, Bruce (2008) *The Search for Al Qaeda: Its Leadership, Ideology, and Future*, Washington DC: Brookings Institution Press.

Robinson, Geoffrey (2010) *'If You Leave Us Here, We Will Die': How Genocide was Stopped in East Timor*, Princeton NJ: Princeton University Press.

Rosenfeld, Michel (2006) 'A Pluralist Theory of Rights in Times of Stress', in W. Sadurski (ed.), *Political Rights Under Stress in 21st Century Europe*, Oxford: Oxford University Press, pp. 12–54.

Roshwald, Aviel (2006) *The Endurance of Nationalism: Ancient Roots and Modern Dilemmas*, Cambridge: Cambridge University Press.

Rousseau, Jean-Jacques (1968) [1762] *The Social Contract and Discourses*, edited by G. D. H. Cole, London: Dent.

Saviano, Roberto (2008), *Gomorrah*, London: Pan Macmillan.

Schmitt, Carl (1988), *The Crisis of Parliamentary Democracy*, translated by Ellen Kennedy, Cambridge MA: MIT Press.

Schmitt, Carl (1996) *The Concept of the Political*, Chicago: Chicago University Press.

Schnapper, D. (1994) *La communauté des citoyens: sur l'idée moderne de nation*, Paris: Gallimard.

Schwarzmantel, John (2003) *Citizenship and Identity: Towards a New Republic*, Abingdon: Routledge.

Schwarzmantel, John (2007) 'Community as Communication: Jean-Luc Nancy and "Being-in-Common"', *Political Studies*, Vol. 55, No. 2, pp. 459–76.

Schwarzmantel, John and H. Kraetzschmar (eds) (2010) *Democracy and Violence*, special issue of *Democratization*, Vol. 17, No. 2.

Slomp, Gabriella (2009) *Carl Schmitt and the Politics of Hostility, Violence and Terror*, Basingstoke: Palgrave Macmillan.

Sloterdijk, Peter (2006) *Zorn und Zeit: Politisch-psychologischer Versuch*, Frankfurt: Suhrkamp Verlag.

Steger, M. B. and N. S. Lind (eds) (1999) *Violence and its Alternatives: An Interdisciplinary Reader*, New York: St. Martin's Press.

Suhrke, Astri (2008) 'Democratising a Dependent State: The Case of Afghanistan', *Democratization*, Vol. 15, No. 3, pp. 630–48.

Tarrow, Sidney (2005) *The New Transnational Activism*, Cambridge: Cambridge University Press.

Tomba, Massimiliano (2009) 'Another Kind of *Gewalt*: Beyond Law: Re-Reading Benjamin', *Historical Materialism*, Vol. 17, No. 1, pp. 126–44.

Touraine, Alain (2000) *Can We Live Together? Equality and Difference*, Cambridge: Polity Press.

Weber, Max (1970) [1919] 'Politics as a Vocation', in *From Max Weber: Essays in Sociology*, edited by H. H. Gerth and C. Wright Mills, London: Routledge & Kegan Paul.

Whitehead, Laurence (2009) 'Losing "the Force"? The "Dark Side" of Democratization After Iraq', *Democratization*, Vol. 16, No. 2, pp. 215–42.

Woodworth, Paddy (2002) *Dirty War, Clean Hands: ETA, the GAL, and Spanish Democracy*, New Haven CT: Yale Nota Bene.

Wydra, H. (2008) 'The Recurrence of Violence', *Sociology Compass*, Vol. 2, No. 1, pp. 183–94.

Young, Iris Marion (2007) 'Power, Violence, and Legitimacy: A Reading of Hannah Arendt in an Age of Police Brutality and Humanitarian Intervention', in Iris Marion Young, *Global Challenges: War, Self-Determination and Responsibility for Justice*, Cambridge: Polity Press.

Index